JOY
IN THE
MOURNING

A MOM'S REFLECTIONS ON A
DECADE IN THE SCHOOL OF GRIEF

DANIELLE ANDERSON

UNITED  HOUSE

ISBN: 978-1-952840-55-5

UNITED HOUSE Publishing
Waterford, Michigan
info@unitedhousepublishing.com
www.unitedhousepublishing.com

Photography:
Lindsey Brittain

Cover Layout and Interior Design:
Matt Russell, Marketing Image, mrussell@marketing-image.com

Printed in the United States of America
2024—First Edition

SPECIAL SALES
Most UNITED HOUSE books are available at special quantity discounts when purchased in bulk by corporations, organizations, and special-interest groups. For information, please e-mail orders@unitedhousepublishing.com

To Jaden, Callen, and Kai -
It's an honor to be your mom.
You think I'm strong, and I need you
to know my strength comes from above,
from the good and loving God, in
whose arms Chase is safe.

But he said to me, "My grace is sufficient for you,
for my power is made perfect in weakness." . . .
For when I am weak, then I am strong.
2 Corinthians 12:9, 10b, NIV

Table of Contents

Foreword

In the depths of our sorrow, we often discover the profound capacity of the human spirit to heal and transcend. Heal, a word of hope dripping with desire to feel whole and restored. In my assessment it seems grief is often the price we pay for love. This book, penned by my wife on her experience after the unexpected loss of our son Chase, delves into the intricate web of emotions that accompany loss. It is a heartfelt guide for those navigating the tumultuous waters of grief, offering solace, understanding, and a roadmap toward healing.

I've seen firsthand how Danielle, as a wife, mother to our four boys, friend and trauma-informed speaker & wellness coach, has helped many of all ages (including yours truly) find the means and methods necessary to heal from trauma and pain. I've benefited from the tenacious effort and knowledge she brings to the world. I can truly say this book is a welcome tool and gift to the reader.

It's often said that those who can't, teach. But Danielle, being the anomaly that she is, is the rarity who not only can do but also can (and should) teach. Every one of her many clients and colleagues would concur. She is well equipped for this task. She has lived through tremendous grief and has put into practice the things she communicates in this book–and we all will be the better for it.

Danielle draws upon the metaphor of a labyrinth to communicate the intricate patterns, winding paths, and complexities of grief. It twists and turns us through the depths of our souls as we navigate sorrow, confusion, and ultimately, transformation. Just as traversing a labyrinth requires patience and perseverance, so too this journey of grief, healing, and restoration.

Grief is a universal experience, yet its impact is deeply personal. It can feel like an isolating journey, leaving us grappling with a myriad of emotions that defy expression. In these moments of darkness, finding a beacon of hope becomes paramount. My wife's expertise shines through these pages, illuminating pathways to navigate grief with resilience and grace. Each chapter gently unravels the layers of grief, offering insights and practical tools for self-discovery and healing.

One of the most poignant aspects of this book is its emphasis on embracing the labyrinth of grief. Though not linear, each small step brings us closer to wholeness–every turn, every detour, is a part of the journey toward healing. Danielle skillfully guides readers through the process of honoring their emotions–even the most painful ones–as stepping stones (pun intended) toward wholeness. In a world that often shies away from grief, her approach fosters a culture of authenticity and acceptance, paving the way for profound healing and growth.

I have seen firsthand the impact of her work. Through her coaching practice, she has guided countless individuals on their journey from grief to resilience, instilling hope and guiding them toward a renewed sense of purpose and joy. I firmly believe that each person who reads this book will become one of the many who will testify in kind.

This book is not just a manual for healing; it is a testament to the resilience of the human spirit. It reminds us that grief, while a formidable force, can also be a catalyst for personal growth and radical change. As you embark on your own journey of self-discovery and healing, may you find solace, wisdom, and renewed hope within these pages.

Through the wisdom shared, you will discover strategies and insights to help you navigate this labyrinth with grace and resilience. It offers a compassionate guide, reminding us that healing is not about forgetting or moving on, but about integrating our experiences into the tapestry of our lives.

May you find solace in the labyrinth, strength in your resilience, and hope in healing.

With heartfelt wishes for your healing journey,
Tedashii

PART 1

My Story

1

Tragedy

Practice Presence: *Take a moment of stillness to breathe deeply to prepare yourself for my terrible story and your reactions and responses. (See Appendix B for suggested breath practices.)*

Thursday morning, March 21, 2013, I was woken up around 5:00 am by Chase screaming from his crib. I ran to check on him. He was burning up. I checked his temperature, and since it was too high for comfort, I raced him to the emergency room. The nurses attended to him, took his temperature, checked his oxygen levels, ran a few other tests, and eventually sent us home with the prescription to keep him cool, hydrated, and give him Tylenol regularly. I followed their advice. We stayed home most of the day. I made a schedule of vitamins, medicines, liquids, broth, and other supplements to give him to prayerfully nurse his little body back to health. We left the house once to drop my husband, Tedashii, who is a musician, off at the airport because he was traveling to a show. He hesitated to leave, but I reassured him we would be okay.

Friday morning found us again in the emergency room; Chase's temperature was even higher than the previous day. This time we left with a prescription for medicine and a machine for breathing treatments. We got home, and I immediately started following a regimen to help him get healthy. He was lethargic and not acting like himself; I prayed for healing and invited many friends and family to do the same. That night I slept in a bed next to Chase's crib, waking every few hours to check his temperature and give him liquids and medicine.

Saturday morning, March 23, Chase was happy. After giving him his first breathing treatment, he smiled and cooed and seemed more like his usual, jolly self. He swatted away the playful, loving, yet bothersome hands of his older brother, Jaden, who was three at the time. I was so grateful.

I laid Chase down for a nap around 10:00 am. About an hour later, I went to wake him to give him water. I always loved seeing him slowly open his eyes, annoyed that someone was waking him from his sleep.

He didn't open his eyes.

I leaned in close to his chest to see if I could hear breathing or a heartbeat, but my heart was pounding so loudly I couldn't tell if it was mine or his. I screamed for my mom. She had come over the night before to help me with Jaden and Chase. She grabbed Chase out of my arms and listened for a heartbeat but couldn't hear one. She said his lips were cold. Terror began to settle into my gut, but I quickly pushed it aside. I needed to stay focused and alert to help my son. I ran him into the living room and started to perform CPR. Someone called 911. Someone else ran Jaden upstairs.

When the ambulance arrived, I felt like a robot, going through the motions, too terrified to let any of my fear settle. Barefoot, I followed the EMTs onto the ambulance. The ride to the hospital was terrible. Chase wasn't breathing. They couldn't find a heartbeat. I just kept praying for the Lord to revive him, let his heart beat, and let him breathe again. Knowing it had been a long time since oxygen had gotten to his brain, I prayed for strength to raise a brain-damaged son.

At the hospital, we were rushed into a room. They laid Chase on a bed and continued their resuscitation attempts. At some point, my mom joined me. We prayed as we looked on with horror at the scene before us.

At 12:17 pm, a lady came over and said, "I'm sorry."

In shock, I screamed and collapsed into my mom. I went over to the bed and rubbed Chase's head. I gave him a kiss. Before I was ready to leave the room, the lady began to usher us into the chapel, asking me questions about insurance and Chase's age. She asked if I'd like to call my pastor. I did.

Paralyzed, my mom reminded me someone needed to call Tedashii. During all the morning terror, he had been on his flight home and was scheduled to land soon. I called. No answer. I left a voicemail, urging him to call me back as soon as he landed. It seemed like in the next moment, he was calling back—which meant it was time for the worst phone call of my life.

I had to tell him Chase didn't make it.

I don't remember much about that call, just him saying over and over, "Don't tell me that. Don't tell me that."

Soon after that horrid phone call, our pastor met us at the hospital and drove my mom and me home. The ride was torture. I couldn't help thinking that I arrived at the hospital as a mom of two, and now I was a mom of one. My mind flashed to the ride home from the birth center one year earlier when Chase was born—it was such a beautiful ride. That day, I was bringing Jaden's little brother home. Now, the inverse was true, and I hated it. I was coming home without Chase.

Much of the first six weeks were foggy. You'll hear more about them in Part 2, but I do remember spending a lot of time journaling—writing with all five senses to capture the fullness of my memories. At the encouragement of a friend, I also found myself constantly praying for what he called a "blessed forgetfulness"—freedom from images that were haunting me and not serving me well. I appreciated this because pictures from the horror of March 23 would randomly flash across my mind. Thankfully, over time, this stopped.

You may be wondering what happened and what the cause was. I've intentionally held back certain parts of the story to keep them sacred, but I will share this. After six weeks, we received the autopsy results. Ugh, I hate having to refer to the truth that my child had an autopsy.

The results were simultaneously frustrating and comforting: "Natural causes."

My first thought was, *What does that even mean?*

I still really don't know.

When discussing it with a friend later, she described it as medical speak for the truth that God numbers our days. At that moment, I both resented and loved her for saying it.

She was right, so I'm choosing to stick with this truth. God numbers our days. As much as I'd like to think I have the power to number the days of my children, I don't. That job is too high and too wonderful for me.

God numbers our days. God numbered Chase's days: 375.

Gentle Reminder

God numbers our days.

Meditation

Take a moment to notice what emotions, sensations, or memories came up for you as you read my story.

Psalm 131, NIV

My heart is not proud, Lord,
my eyes are not haughty;
I do not concern myself with great matters
or things too wonderful for me.

But I have calmed and quieted myself,
I am like a weaned child with its mother;
like a weaned child I am content.
Israel, put your hope in the Lord
both now and forevermore.

(2)

Celebrating Chase

"All go to one place. All are from the dust,
and to dust all return."
Ecclesiastes 3:20, ESV

Thursday, March 28, 2013, five days after tragedy struck, we had the services.

That morning I got dressed to go to a cemetery. I put on my dress and aquamarine shoes, new items I bought for Chase's Celebration service. Aquamarine is his birthstone, and what I now like to call his lifestone. I combed through my new haircut. I put a little makeup on, even though I knew I'd cry through it in the next few hours. I sat on the bed in a partial fog, realizing this would be the second hardest, the second worst day of my life. I headed out the door. Someone told me I looked nice. I didn't care.

In the car to the funeral home, I sat in a daze, my face frozen behind my new prescription sunglasses from Sam's. Chase was sitting in the grocery cart when I chose these sunglasses a little over a week ago. Now I'm about to get into a funeral home limo and be transported to his graveside service.

I hate this.

When we arrived at the cemetery for the private graveside service, I frantically looked for the green canopy that marked where our little group would meet. I needed to find it because it would be a reference for finding the item I didn't want to see, but one I had to—a little casket.

Once my eyes locked on the casket, I broke down in tears, but I also felt a sense of relief—*it was not as small as I expected.*

Hard, yet comforting, truths were shared at this service. Our friend, Adam, compared life to waiting in line at an amusement park. He said Chase got to skip the line—Chase was experiencing the joy we all longed for in our hearts. This was comforting.

Later, I found a quote from a pastor that said, "And he will thank you for giving him life. He will thank you for enduring the loss, that he might have the reward sooner."

Chase got the reward sooner.

Pastor Matt explained though we are afflicted in every way, we are not crushed. We get to be confused. We get to ask questions, but we are never driven to despair. We have hope.

Our worship leader and a vocalist from church played "Never Once" by Matt Redman. We cried through the entire song. This was the song Chase was born to, and now, it was the song shared on the day of his burial. The song became bitter, as well as sweet, and served as bookends for his life here on earth.

A harsh sting and a terrible horror enveloped me that day. There was something wrong with seeing the beginning and end of someone's life. Something was wrong with being so intimately aware of one person's journey from dust to dust. I pushed him out at birth. I got to experience Chase coming from dust—from my body. And that day we knew our baby was returning to dust.

I didn't realize it then, but a close friend, Ashley, later told me when Tedashii and I were dismissed to go back to the limo after the service, she saw me look up and smile. I believe this quote I found later by Robert L. Dabney explains why.

"As I stand by the little grave, and think of the poor ruined clay within, that was a few days ago so beautiful, my heart bleeds."

This is the harsh sting.

The quote continues, "But as I ask, 'Where is the soul whose beams gave that clay all its beauty and preciousness?' I triumph."[2]

This is the constant tension I live in.

I have a bleeding heart. Death makes me have a bleeding heart. There's something wrong with it. It was not a part of God's original, good creation. Death came as a result of sin.

But God also gives me a triumphant heart. I have confidence that Chase is safe in the arms of God. I triumph because I know I will see him again.

After the graveside service, we headed to the church for what we now call Chase's Celebration Service—the word funeral still seems too ugly, too harsh. Rather than dark hues, we asked people to wear aquamarine. It was going to be a sad, terribly tragic service. At the same time, I knew there would be a celebration—a celebration of Chase's life, and a celebration that he was safe with the Father.

Pastor Beau spoke. He read 1 Thessalonians 4:13-14, ESV, "But we do not want you to be uninformed, brothers, about those who are asleep, that you may not grieve as others do who have no hope. For since we believe that Jesus died and rose again, even so, through Jesus, God will bring with him those who have fallen asleep." He reminded us that though we will grieve and should continue to do so, we can grieve as those with hope.

He then shared some "words from Mom" I gave him before the service, knowing I wouldn't have the energy nor the strength to address the crowd. My words, through Beau, were to build your house on the Rock, an encouragement to believe God is all He says He is, an encouragement to do work with the Lord now, and beg Him for help to believe His truth—about Himself and you. I knew there would be peace and comfort if we leaned into this Rock of Ages, the God of all comfort. I didn't know how peace would come or what comfort would look like during such excruciating pain, but I knew God didn't lie.

Since that day, celebrating Chase has become something we have baked into our lives. We include a picture of him when we take our annual family pictures, and we hang up his Christmas stocking on the mantle (ugh, he only got one Christmas). Whenever my friend, Tricia, and I get together with all of our kids (which usually happens only once a year), we line up the kids in birth order for a picture and always leave a "space for Chase." His birthday is a larger celebration. Friends join us at the park for a balloon release, Chase Muffins (gluten-free banana muffins), Greek yogurt, and strawberries. Chase enjoyed this when he turned one, so we enjoy it every year in remembrance of him. Our family and friends outside Atlanta do their own balloon releases and send us videos.

Another regular activity at the park is flipping through Chase's photo albums. I proudly lay them on a picnic table and encourage friends to flip through and ask me questions—eager to tell stories and talk about him. Chase's lifestone color, aquamarine, has become a staple in my wardrobe, jewelry, home decor, and even logos and presentations—this is true for my mom and sister as well.

We talk about Chase as a family. We watch videos and listen as Jaden shares his memories and questions. Callen and Kai are free to ask questions as well, and they know they have an older brother they haven't met. On the anniversary of Chase's passing, what we call his Glory Day, we keep an open calendar, cautious to plan activities because we've discovered that each year brings with it some unpredictable emotions. This is usually the date that if any activity happens, it happens with family or a small set of trusted friends.

Yes, we celebrate, and yes, we still miss Chase.

Gentle Reminder

Celebration and sorrow can co-exist.

Meditation

*What ways of celebrating your
child would serve you well?*

My Sweetums

Blog post originally dated August 14, 2013,

It seems that as soon as you announce your pregnancy, a shift takes place in the types of questions people ask you. Before, you were asked about marriage or how work was going; after, suddenly, all the questions start to center around the baby in your womb.

When I first announced my pregnancy with Jaden, someone told me to enjoy my last few months of people asking about me because as soon as that baby got here, I'd get pushed to the back burner, and the questions I'd answer would be about my child.

I was okay with the shift. I loved answering questions about Jaden. And still do.

The shift continued when I announced my pregnancy with Chase. And again, I loved it! Once he was born, I loved answering "How are the boys?" and "What new things is Chase doing this week?" questions.

Sadly, I don't get to answer many questions about Chase anymore. People are starting to ask questions about me again. I appreciate the care and concern, it's just that sometimes it feels so foreign. I haven't had to talk about myself so much in almost four years.

I want to talk about my Sweetums. So in honor of what would have been Chase turning seventeen months, I'm going to talk about him.

Chase was such a chill baby. From the day he was born, he really didn't cry unless he was hungry—but when he was hungry, you knew. He had a pretty hefty appetite, going from 6 lbs 14 oz to 13 lbs 15 oz in eight weeks! He doubled his birth weight in two months. (I think the goal is to do that by six months, so he was ahead of the game!)

Celebrating Chase

Around four months, Chase started to drool uncontrollably. He wouldn't get his first tooth until seven months, right around Thanksgiving, but he was just juicy! I have many pictures and videos where he's just as happy as can be playing with his toys, wearing a completely drenched shirt or bib. In case you missed it, it was drenched because of his slobber.

You won't find many pictures of him with his mouth closed. I'm not sure why that is, but I always blamed it on his JBL (juicy bottom lip). I am convinced it was just weighing him down. We have a few pictures with his mouth closed; in them, he's either sleeping or has something in his mouth. I really loved looking at his juicy little open mouth. Sometimes I'd just put the tip of my nose in it to steal a nose kiss. Once he learned to give kisses, I'd gladly await the slobbery goodness coming for me.

In March, Chase had really started to get around the house. He had crawling down and was becoming a master climber. He'd climb on top of his Lego box, step stools, and whatever else he could find. He could scale the stairs like a champ and was beginning to learn how to come back down. (Usually, once he reached the landing at the top, he'd just sit there because he wasn't confident in coming down.) He could stand up for about ten seconds, and then he'd just fall down. I think he was so close to walking! I estimated he'd start around thirteen-and-a-half months.

I was told that along with grieving the loss of your child, you grieve your dreams, hopes, and predictions. And those are painful to grieve too.

I used to sit Chase in his high chair in front of the TV to watch "Your Baby Can Read" DVDs. When Jaden was a baby, he would watch these easily, quickly picking up on the words. Chase, not so much. That boy would not focus on the screen. He'd turn his whole body around in the high chair to see what else was going on. Sometimes I'd sit and hold him, thinking he may be more still in my arms. Nope. He was always trying to crawl away. He couldn't care less about the words on the screen or even the songs. He did eventually learn to put his "arms up" when told, and when he saw the words on the screen or a card, I was convinced Chase was the child who would just need a little more encouragement in school.

I imagined sitting down with a five-year-old Jaden and a three-year-old Chase to read a book. Jaden, who began reading at three, would read his page with excitement and ease. He'd then say, "Your turn, Chase," and Chase would just rip the page or run away.

I pictured the boys being great buddies as they grew older together. They were going to be partners. Jaden would be long and lean; he'd be the performer. Chase was going to be the big little brother, tall but wide and stout and very strong; he'd be the bouncer. He wouldn't have many words for you, the silent type, but he'd get you if you got in his, or his brother's, way.

That's my Sweetums. Oh, how I miss him.

Gentle Reminder

"What is grief, if not love persevering?"
Vision, Wandavision[3]

Meditation

Take a moment to remember some of your favorite
moments and memories of the child you lost.
As much as possible, allow all five senses to be
involved. What sights, smells, sounds, tastes,
and textures were involved? Write down
anything you'd like to capture.

Sound Healing

"You're the Best Song" by Bethany Dillon. I refer
to this song as my "mommy song" and used to sing
it to Chase. I encourage you to look it up and listen
to its beautiful lyrics.

(See Appendix A for helpful postures
you can take while listening.)

(3)

Words from Mom

Everyone then who hears these words of mine and does them will be like a wise man who built his house on the rock. And the rain fell, and the floods came, and the winds blew and beat on that house, but it did not fall, because it had been founded on the rock. And everyone who hears these words of mine and does not do them will be like a foolish man who built his house on the sand. And the rain fell, and the floods came, and the winds blew and beat against that house, and it fell, and great was the fall of it.
Matthew 7:24-27, ESV

While we were organizing the order of service for the Celebration, I deeply desired to share some things the Lord had made very clear to me in those first days of our nightmare. I wanted to include "Words from Mom" in his service because I thought people may want to hear from me. I thought a question many people would have was, "What is Danielle thinking?" or "If Danielle could give some advice after this experience, what would she say?"

Maybe some would expect me to say something like, "Hug your babies more" or "The time you get with your children is so sweet and so short; cherish it all you can." Maybe others would expect me to encourage them to pray with their children more and train them in such a way as to avoid any regrets.

I hugged and kissed Chase all the time. I quit my job at Accenture as an act of obedience, believing the Lord was asking me to give my time, especially in those early formative years, to my children. I prayed over Chase every night, so he would constantly be bombarded with the truth of the gospel. Every night, I sang each verse of the popular hymn *In Christ Alone* before he went to sleep. I nursed him, played with him, read to him, and did learning time with him—and I don't have any regrets.

"Yes" and "Amen" to all these things. I think they are highly valuable and important. But my "Words from Mom" would not center around any of these things. In fact, they wouldn't center around Chase at all.

They would center around the triune God of the Bible—Adonai. Ha'Shem—The Name—Father, Son, and Holy Spirit.

In short, my "Words from Mom" were, and still are, an encouragement for you to believe that God is all He says He is. They're an encouragement to do work with the Lord now and begging for help to believe His truth—about God and you.

Knowing I played with Chase as often as possible didn't give me a peace that surpasses all understanding after he passed—that is a grace gift from the Lord.

Teaching Chase some words in sign language didn't protect my heart as I played "What If?" games in my mind after he passed—that is a grace gift from the Lord.

Nursing Chase as long as I could, didn't give me hope I'll see him again—that is a grace gift from the Lord.

For the past decade, as I continue to learn more about God and Heaven, my new world to come, through scripture, books, podcasts, and sermons, I ask myself, "Do I believe this?" And not "Do I just cognitively agree with this XYZ statement?", but "Do I live in such a way that shows I believe XYZ to be true?"

Words from Mom

Here are some examples of questions I've had to wrestle through:

- "Do I really believe that God cannot lie?" (Titus 1:1)
- "Do I really believe that God is good?" (Psalm 119:68)
- "Do I really believe that children are ultimately the Lord's and that they are gifts entrusted to parents for a season (however long or short)?" (Psalm 127:3)
- "Do I really believe that God is working all things for the good of those who love Him?" (Romans 8:28)

This practice has not been easy. Though I give effort, it's a grace-enabled effort allowing me to choose and believe the truth. With each choice to believe the truth, it's like an added pad of defense for my mind. In my life, God has proven to be the Solid Rock, and He's been building my foundation on Him. He's been preparing me to handle the storms better—because they will come.

Of course, there are days I struggle with this. That's part of the human experience. I no longer subscribe to the illusion of perfection. There are days when my thoughts, or the Enemy's lies, lead me down a path away from God's truth. But God, through the Spirit and often through the means of close friends or family, reminds me what is true.

So I beg you to believe that God is who He says He is. I plead with you to believe that He cannot lie and that His word is truth.

I still stand by the "Words from Mom" shared at Chase's Celebration Service - build your house on the Rock.

→ What's your response?

Gentle Reminder

God cannot lie. God is forever trustworthy.

Meditation

What stories do you tell yourself about God's goodness and trustworthiness? What's one thing that will help you believe God is who He says He is?

Interlude - Sound Healing

Listen to the song "How He Loves" by David Crowder Band or Anthony Evans. Take a moment to note anything that stood out during your listening.

(See Appendix A for helpful postures you can take while listening.)

Words from Mom

He Loves Us, He Loves Me

Excerpt from a blog post originally dated July 2013,

A beautiful truth—that God loves me—has begun to take center stage in my life.

I have known God loved me for a long time, but I honestly haven't let it sink into every fiber in the fabric of my being. If you asked me if I felt loved by God, there was hesitation. I realize I didn't fully believe God's love for me. That is sobering and sad. I have begun to reread scriptures about God's love, ones I thought I knew so well, and it's like I am reading them for the first time. They breathe life in a way they never have before. I read other well-known scriptures, ones I never saw as relating to love, and now they seem to scream God's steadfast, unfailing love.

At some level, I understood how foundational the truth of God's love is. After all, God is love. But God is opening my eyes and heart to experience this anchoring truth in a brand new, amazing way.

And oh, how my heart needs it in the midst of loss.

Before I continue with my reflections, let me take a moment to tell you God loves you. If no one has reminded you of that recently, I'm sorry. I'll gladly be a voice to remind you: you are loved by God. I need us both to anchor in the truth that we are loved, and God delights in us (Numbers 6)—even in the midst of heartache. Nothing can change this.

As I reflect on these years of grief, I can see how I began them with a perspective of seeing God more as a judge than a loving father. I was hesitant to accept that God loved me—I saw it as wrong, selfish, and too me-centered. Over the years, this has shifted.

When was the last time you reminded yourself that God loves you? That God delights in you? The human experience has convinced us that we have been separated from God. A Bible study I have been studying with friends for the last few years teaches that the idea of being separated from God is the great illusion of this "world of concealment." The study reminds us how our spirit came from God and descended into this world of concealment. When we die, our spirit will leave this world and return to God (Ecclesiastes 12:7). Part of our job in this world of concealment is to remind ourselves that God is always present, and since God is love, this means love is always present. We need this truth more than ever in times of pain, grief, sorrow, and loss. There are times when God feels far and distant. In those moments, we can remind ourselves that God is very near, and God loves us.

Because this is true, when it comes to love, I have come to embrace an abundance mentality: there is more than enough love to go around. Which is music to sorrowful ears.

Sadly, it seems our culture teaches an opposing view rooted in a scarcity mentality: love is a limited resource. If that's true, we will definitely find ourselves entering into the game of comparative suffering. Have you ever done this? Discounting your pain because someone else in the world, or history, faced something you deemed harder or worse? *She lost her mom and daughter in the car accident. I just lost my child, so I shouldn't be as sad.* Or maybe you've discounted your pain because of your relational proximity. *I'm just the aunt; that was her child. I shouldn't be this sad.*

The good news is that love is abundant. There is enough room, enough love, enough empathy, and enough understanding for my story and yours—my pain and yours. We can hold space for both. This means your story does not have to invalidate my pain, and my story does not have to invalidate yours. Love exists in abundance because God is love, and we ought to have permission to sit in its abundance, whether we are grieving or not.

I don't know about you, but the church tradition I come from lets the pendulum swing too far on the side of sin and evil. I was first a sinner in need of God's grace. That's a scarcity mentality, a shame-first gospel message that begins my story in Genesis 3 rather than Genesis 1. Let me explain.

Genesis 3 is the account of what we commonly refer to as The Fall. It tells the story of Eve's deception by the serpent and Adam & Eve's subsequent exile from the garden because of their disobedience. If the narrative opens in Genesis 3, it starts with a lens of disobedience, sin, and deficit. But that's not where my story, or yours, begins. It originates in Genesis 1, where we are reminded that a *good* God created a *good* creation. This good creation is filled with beauty and order. And the "crown" of this creation are human beings—made in the image of this good God—with wholeness, value, and dignity.

It's in this Genesis 1 posture I choose to stand—confident, knowing I am a loved, beautiful creation of God, made in God's image with a purpose.

→What's your response?

Gentle Reminder

The steadfast love of The Lord never ceases;
his mercies never come to an end; they are new
every morning; great is your faithfulness.
Lamentations 3:22-23, ESV, emphasis added

For this reason, I bow my knees before the Father,
from whom every family in heaven and on earth is
named, that according to the riches of his glory he
may grant you to be strengthened with power through
his Spirit in your inner being, so that Christ may dwell in
your hearts through faith-that you, being rooted and
grounded in love, may have strength to comprehend
with all the saints what is the breadth and length and
height and depth, and to know the love of Christ
that surpasses knowledge, that you may be filled
with all the fullness of God.
Ephesians 3:14-19, ESV

But I have trusted in your steadfast love; my
heart shall rejoice in your salvation. I will sing to
the LORD, because he has dealt bountifully with me.
Psalm 13:5-6, ESV, emphasis added

Words from Mom

Meditation

God's Love Breath Practice

*The scriptures say God breathed into you the breath
of life. It's been said that God's very name YHWH
is the sound of the breath.*

*Take at least one minute to breathe deeply, and remind
yourself of God's presence and love with every breath.*

Held Body Practice

*This practice will involve you finding a comfortable
position. You could choose to be seated in a chair or
on the floor, lying on the floor or on a bed. Refer to
Appendix A for body posture ideas. Whatever position
you choose, get comfortable and plan to maintain
that posture of stillness for at least five minutes.*

*Once you have found your posture of stillness, gently
begin to bring your awareness to the breath. Notice
if it is deep or shallow. Then take three slow, deep breaths.
After that, allow your breath to be what it is (no need
to control it), and send your awareness to the parts of
your body making contact with the ground, bed, chair,
or any supports underneath you. Become fully aware
of the sensation of being held and supported. As you*

PART 2

Reflections

Ache

A journal entry dated April 23, 2013,

Today is a milestone I never wanted to celebrate—one month of us being without Chase. My heart bleeds and triumphs at the same time. I miss him like crazy. I want him back. I want to play with him, hold him, kiss him, and I know I can't—my heart bleeds.

Then I remember he is safe in the arms of the Father, singing praises to King Jesus. He is safe and happy, he'll never know pain or sorrow—ever. He is experiencing never-ending joy—my heart triumphs.

I read a blog yesterday. It was a letter written to a mom who had a stillborn son—and it was very helpful. It accurately described the pain of grief—it's similar to that of losing a body part— you have the initial pain of the loss and the continued pain of the gone-ness. Then it wrote about what Chase would say on That Day when we are reunited. He will thank me for giving him life, and he will thank me for enduring the loss, the pain, so he might have the reward sooner.

Phrased that way somehow makes the pain more bearable. I'm glad, in some way, that Chase won't endure loss, and he can have the reward. I'm glad the pain I feel is somehow for his benefit. I know the pain will last forever—there will be an ache, but the ache doesn't have to rule. So far, the ache has been huge and overwhelming at times, but it is not ruling. And I thank the God of all comfort for that.

④

Bleeding Heart

Practice Presence: *Take a moment of stillness to breathe deeply to prepare yourself to be present with my words and your reactions and responses. (See Appendix B for suggested breath practices.)*

Anguish.
Heartache.
Agony.
Horror.
Terror.
Trauma.

I never expected these to become regular parts of my life, but they have. My heart hurts every day—some days are less intense than others, but it still hurts. Little stings throughout the day that I just have to live with.

It sucks.

Though I have learned to find joy in this terrible journey, I want to be honest about the truth that it is terrible.

In the beginning, I think I mostly lived in a state of horror. The Oxford Dictionary defines horror as an intense feeling of fear, shock, or disgust.

Yes, fear, shock, and disgust were real, however, the loss didn't feel real. It couldn't be real. But it was real—because Chase wasn't there.

There was a forever hole in my heart that I couldn't fix.

Chase being gone and the finality of knowing he wasn't coming back was excruciating. I don't even know how many days straight I sobbed and screamed in the shower. And then a day came, maybe two weeks in, where I felt numb. I was tired of crying, tired of feeling the pain that came with the loss, and I figured I deserved a break.

The pain was unbearable, and there was no way I was going to be able to live every day like this. And on top of my pain, there were realities around me that seemed to compound it. I was a mom to a 3-year-old boy who needed me and had questions about his brother. I was a wife to a man with his own responses to trauma who seemed to require more from me than I could give. I was a grieving woman who had to shield dumb comments and questions from those in and out of the community. I was being asked to extend grace and offer the benefit of the doubt when they said asinine things.

Life felt cruel. God felt cruel.

I could not live like this. I had to figure something out. Living this way wasn't sustainable; it felt unbearable. I needed help to stop the bleeding. So I began to contemplate my drug of choice. Prior to grief, I'd describe myself as extremely judgmental and self-righteous, not understanding why an adult would choose to live their life constantly numbed by drugs and alcohol. I'd think to myself, *That doesn't make any sense; just make a different choice.*

After March 23, 2013, it made sense. I could empathize. I understood. *Life sucks. It hurts. I get why you don't want to feel this. I don't want to feel this. I don't want to be here. Lord, just take me too. Let me just go be with Chase.*

Life was dark. I felt like giving up, like leaving. Knowing I didn't have it in me to end my life, I decided I could at least select a "drug of choice" that would allow me to numb out. *Lord, help me find something that can be my escape and shield me from the depths of this pain.*

How about drugs? I'd never taken illegal drugs in my life, so that didn't feel like an option.

What about alcohol? I also wasn't the biggest fan of alcohol; I was afraid if I drank too much, I'd throw up—and I hate throwing up.

So what would I turn to? What would make me happy and help me escape—moments and maybe eventually life?

Sugar.

Yes, that's it. I'll eat myself to death.

Sugar became my drug of choice–I resolved to escape into cookies, gummy bears, and ice cream when the pain seemed unbearable. It seemed like a decent choice as it would allow me to parent, wife, and function in other relationships. *This seems like a win-win. I won't be high or drunk. I can take care of my responsibilities, and I won't have to feel this pain. Yes, please.*

That didn't last long.

Not even four weeks into grieving Chase, I found out I was pregnant. This news came with mixed emotions:

- Confusion - *What the hell?*
- Disdain - *I don't want this baby. I want Chase.*
- Sadness - *Ugh, I miss Chase. I remember what it was like when I found out I was pregnant with him.*
- Helplessness - *How am I going to grieve while pregnant?*
- Fear - *Can I grow a healthy baby? Or will this end in miscarriage or death after a year too?*
- Paralysis - *I don't know what to do.*

After I told Tedashii, I called my midwife, Jean. I don't remember all that she said, but the main takeaway was: *your grief will affect this baby; as best you can, let yourself feel what you need to feel and cry when you need to cry.*

Well great.

This is exactly what I don't want to do. I don't want to feel. Feeling hurts.

→ What's your response?

Bleeding Heart

Gentle Reminder

*It's OK if your grief feels unbearable.
Your life is worth living. God travels
with you through the tunnel.*

Meditation

*Emotions are like tunnels; you have to travel through
them to get to the light on the other side. What's
one tunnel of emotion you have to travel through?
Name it and say it out loud. What can you do to make
a little forward progress through the tunnel? If you
need support, reach out to someone you trust or
imagine God's presence with you as you travel.*

Interlude - Sound Healing

*Listen to the song "Thy Will" by Hilary Scott.
Take a moment to note anything that stood out
during your listening.*

*(See Appendix A for helpful postures
you can take while listening.)*

Struck Down

Excerpt from a journal entry dated May 23, 2013,

*Two months. Two months since I've held Chase.
Two months since I've kissed him. I miss him like
crazy. The pain, at times, is unbearable . . . I wouldn't
wish this on my worst enemy. Today wasn't as painful
as I expected, but lies have been creeping in this
week about me contributing to Chase's death . . .*

*Maybe I set him up at a disadvantage in life because
I had Group B strep. But I had loving friends who
boldly declared that as a lie and firmly told me to fight
it, to be fierce against it. And by God's grace, for the past
two days, I have. I did not cause Chase's death—his
days were numbered well before my milk supply changed
and well before I had Group B strep. So today, I choose
to rest in the truth that God's plans are more wise and
way better than my own. He ordained today—a day
where I'd mourn the two-month absence of my baby
boy. The GriefShare email today was right on time—
I have been forcefully struck down, but I am not
destroyed (2 Corinthians 4:9).*

*I miss pressing my cheek up against his—it was so
soft. I miss his juicy kisses and the softness of his
big lips. I want to experience that now. But I can't.
I'm struck down, but not destroyed.*

(5)

The New Normal

Practice Presence: *Take a moment of stillness to breathe deeply to prepare yourself to be present with my words and your reactions and responses. (See Appendix B for suggested breath practices.)*

Ah, the infamous "new normal." I've never liked this phrase; there is nothing normal about doing life without Chase.

Side note: If you're like me, and you don't like this common phrase, feel free to get creative and adopt a new phrase to serve you better, like new rhythms or new patterns.

Deep breath. Hard truth loading → You don't have to like it, but you will have to learn to accept this new way of life. It took a while for the newness to sink in. In my mind, "new" comes with a positive connotation—something shiny and better than a previous version or iteration. Nothing felt better about Chase not being there. I struggled to squeeze myself into this new way of life. It felt like a chore, and I didn't want it anyway—just like in 5th grade when my mom would make me try on dresses that didn't fit at the store. *Can we leave now? I just want to go home and read my books.*

Somehow I had to make this fit; I had to learn it. I had to get used to putting only one son to bed at night, strapping one son into a car seat, and no longer changing diapers. I had to say "Jaden" rather than "the boys" and it hurt. "I'm taking *Jaden* to the park." "I'm going to the store with *Jaden*." I missed getting the boys dressed for church and hearing the precious harmonies of two crying children as I tried to brush my teeth and put on clothes not stained with drool and food.

Ugh, I wanted the plural back. The boys. My sons. Eventually, I would get the "s" back, and even though it brought a sense of relief, as you can expect, there was still a sting because Chase wasn't here.

It was hard to adjust. In those early months, I had to watch Jaden play by himself. I no longer had a baby on my lap when I read him a bedtime story.

Every day at 1:00 pm, I was at a loss. I didn't know what to do with myself. "Normal" was to put Jaden down for a nap and then do solo learning time with Chase before his second nap at 1:30 pm. But now, Chase was gone, Jaden was asleep, Tedashii was distant, and I was alone. I didn't know much about trauma and the nervous system in 2013, but I know a lot now. And I know loss is a huge hit–to you and your nervous system. Let me use an example to make this point better.

Imagine it's a gorgeous, sunny day, and you're outside on the top deck of a cruise ship, enjoying the beauty of still waters. We'll call this homeostasis—the calm, "rest and digest" state of your nervous system. There are no dark clouds or churning water to warn you. Out of nowhere, a violent storm hits and throws you overboard, and you are unequipped and untrained to deal with such an event.

In the example, you're not a trained water rescue person. Though you may be able to swim, this situation is jarring and terrifying. This storm is a trauma. Resmaa Menakem[4] states trauma can be created by things that are "too much, too fast, too soon." And when facing a trauma, the nervous system doesn't immediately bounce back. In the same way that once you land in the water, you don't find yourself instantaneously back at the top of the ship—once again enjoying the gorgeous, sunny day.

The New Normal

The nervous system would love to return to its homeostasis state, but other immediate things have to be dealt with first. When you've been knocked into the water, your way back to homeostasis includes going through the storm. The nervous system has several jobs, but its primary one is keeping you safe and alive. In this example, I'm sure the first thing the nervous system does when it realizes it is in the water is to begin to figure out how to be safe in the water:

Can I swim?

What's close to me that I can hold on to?

Is there someone who can throw me a life vest?

What did my swim coach say was the number one safety skill? Oh, yeah— backfloat.

But what if there are sharks? Maybe I should swim.

There are so many variables the nervous system has to take in, sort, and find meaning to, and then it must determine and initiate the appropriate action. Once that's figured out, then there's the issue of deciding how to get back to the ship:

Is swimming back to the ship an option?

Is there a life raft available?

Is there a lifeguard somewhere who sees me? If so, do they have the tools to get me out?

You could keep this example going—figuring out what to do once you're back on the ship, yet still so far from the peace and calm you were experiencing at the top level before the storm threw you overboard.

Living with loss and learning to adjust to the new is a lot like this. Sometimes it feels like sheer survival. Be patient with yourself as you make your way from the water to a raft and back to the bottom deck of the cruise ship. At some point, you will probably return to the top deck, but you will forever be changed. Your experience of the top deck will never be what it was before the storm hit. Partly because you are a different person, and now you have lived through the experience of knowing a storm can come out of nowhere.

Rest and calm, settling into a new routine, and homeostasis is a possibility, both in your body and in your life. Though you may come to it kicking and screaming, you will learn a different, new way of living. It may feel unwelcome and unwanted, but sadly, it will come. It will probably include new ways of thinking, doing, and even relating to others. You will be a different person.

I remember lamenting to a mom who was further down the journey than me. I shared how I felt like everywhere I went, people looked at me as the grieving mom. It was as if I had a letter stamped on my chest, like the woman in *The Scarlet Letter* who was forced to sew a scarlet-colored "A" on her bodice as punishment for her adulterous affair. She understood the sentiment and validated me—I had been marked. She had too. And so have you.

Though it's a letter I never wanted to wear, she said I got to choose how I would wear it; I got to choose what I would do with it. And that's true of you too. There's no rush—take as much time as you need to figure out what works for you. Use trial and error. Scream and cry. Throw a tantrum.

I believe you will learn you can hold both joy and sorrow in tension as you discover what life looks like on this side of loss.

→ What's your response?

The New Normal

Gentle Reminder

You don't have to like the "new normal," but you will have to learn to accept it.

Meditation

I mentioned I was at a loss at 1 PM, which was intentional Chase and me time. Is there a part of your new routine you feel especially lost in? If so, consider what might serve you well as you create and learn a new routine.

For example, my 1 PM took on different iterations in that first year of grief. Some days it was a time to rest, and others it was a time to read, journal, or pray. Some days it was just me looking at pictures of Chase and letting myself cry. To help myself have flexibility during that time and not feel like I had to do the same thing every day, I kept a list on my phone of suggested activities. When I needed support determining something to do, I would look at the list.

Here are some activities to consider incorporating into your routine: practice intentional stillness or silence to check in with yourself, journal, listen to a sermon or podcast, read a book, call a friend or family member, work on a memory book, take a nap, find a way to laugh, or sit outside.

(6)

Griefs and Sorrows

Surely he has borne our griefs and carried our sorrows;
Isaiah 53:4, ESV

*And when Jesus entered Peter's house, he saw his
mother-in-law lying sick with a fever. He touched her
hand, and the fever left her, and she rose and began to
serve him. That evening they brought to him many who
were oppressed by demons, and he cast out the spirits
with a word and healed all who were sick. This was
to fulfill what was spoken by the prophet Isaiah: "He
took our illnesses and bore our diseases."*
Matthew 8:14-17, ESV

Practice Presence: *Take a moment of stillness to breathe
deeply to prepare yourself to be present with my words and
your reactions and responses. (See Appendix B for suggested
breath practices.)*

In December 2013, while going through our church's Advent guide, I discovered these two scripture references. As I studied more, I was amazed to find out the Hebrew words for griefs and sorrows in Isaiah 53, respectively, could also mean sickness and pains, illnesses and diseases; words found in Matthew 8. It led to an aha moment.

My grief is a sickness.

Since the terrible day in March 2013, Tedashii and I had constantly described ourselves as weak. We had a diminished capacity and bandwidth, and we felt like we had lost a limb, a leg; we felt broken and needed help learning to walk again. It was strangely encouraging to have these ideas validated by the truth of scripture.

We were sick. We needed healing.

You're not lazy. You're grieving.

I believe God is the ultimate, capital H, Healer, and I look forward to That Day when the Healer, who sent a weeping Son, will wipe away our tears. But That Day is not here yet, so I need some help in the now.

I've found the idea of "grief sickness" to not be socially acceptable. And it's not easily understood. But with fresh insight from the Lord, I found myself experiencing more freedom to ask for what I needed. It gave me more courage to say yes and no to various things. If I had been diagnosed with a physical sickness and had to adjust my schedule to fit in time for treatments, I would do it without hesitation. And others around me would understand. Even though I may not have looked physically ill, I was hurt and had to make time for my "treatments." I was all the more motivated to do so because another child was growing in my body. I didn't know how it would work, but if there was a chance to lessen the impact my grief had on his little brain and body, I wanted to reduce it as much as possible.

I began to refer to the various activities I intentionally participated in as my treatment plan. This treatment plan, or "care package," as one of my students calls it, has had many iterations over the years. Initially, when the pain was most intense, it felt like I was in triage. This was when I had the least amount of energy, so caring for myself was drinking a smoothie (because chewing seemed exhausting), taking a shower, and learning how to be present with my emotions. As my energy increased, I was able to add working out, talking with family and friends, and taking a laughter vitamin (watching a funny show) to my treatment plan.

The intensity continued to lessen over time. At some point, the plan shifted from triage into a more vitamin-like maintenance plan, something to take proactively to maintain my capacity and help me face what was to come. Eventually, I began to adopt this worldview, the idea of needing a care package in all of life. I needed intentional practices to help me know and experience God and the abundant life God had made available, including comfort and healing.

Another scripture that fueled my pursuit of healing in grief is Deuteronomy 30:19, AMP, which says, "I call heaven and earth as witnesses against you today, that I have set before you life and death, the blessing and the curse; therefore, you shall choose life in order that you may live, you and your descendants."

It seemed to speak directly to my desire—I want to live, and I want this baby in my womb to live too—and I quickly applied it to my care package. The key lesson for me was this—I had a choice, which meant I had a choice in how I would navigate grief. As I meditated on the scripture, the picture that came to mind was one of a fork in the road. I saw one side of the fork in the road leading to all that is God's abundant life, God's Kingdom of Shalom, and I was reminded it is available now, not just in the World to Come. Surprisingly, I was obviously in a season where I was very aware of the reality of death as mentioned in the verse. But I did not see it as bodily, physical death. Instead, I saw that side of the fork in the road leading to anything that wasn't God's abundant life. This road led to strife, chaos, and confusion, which were common in the world's systems. If joy meant life, then despair meant death. If hope meant life, then hopelessness meant death. If acceptance meant life, then resentment meant death. Got it—let me update my treatment plan accordingly.

This has become my way of life—knowing I have a choice at every moment. I can choose joy or despair. I can choose hope or hopelessness. I can choose to engage with what I am feeling, or I can suppress it. Armed with this knowledge and the truth that God has given me everything I need for life and godliness, I am better equipped for this unpredictable journey of grief. As a sojourner on this path for a decade and a participant in therapy (Bless God for therapy!), I have learned I can easily be consciously or unconsciously triggered by something. When that's the case, I'm gentle with myself and remember my treatment plan. Maybe I need to go cry, take a nap, reach out to someone for help, or cancel the rest of the day's obligations.

One Saturday evening in September 2020, we'd enjoyed playing a fun family game of kickball with several families in our community, and we were heading to a friend's house for s'mores. I don't fully remember what was said, but on the drive over, one of my sons asked an innocent question about Chase. I was thrown off by the question and could feel a tightening in my body and an immediate feeling of wanting to go home. I fought the urge because I wanted to give my kids a chance to enjoy friends and eat sweets, so I, instead, awkwardly sat around a firepit, taking deep breaths, trying my best to hold back tears.

After one round of s'mores, I chose to enact the part of the treatment plan that permits me to leave difficult social settings. It was time for me to go home, cry in the shower, lay down, and cancel any other plans on the calendar that night. I explained to a few of the moms what had happened and that I needed to go home. They understood, helped me get the boys together, and I went home.

Vulnerability is an important, though difficult, part of the treatment plan. I need the courage to admit what I'm feeling and the courage to express it. I often refer to this practice of vulnerability in the face of grief as "leaning into the wave of sorrow." When practicing vulnerability, it's also nice to have people around who will accept me rather than dismiss or ignore me. Thankfully, on the night around the fire pit, I had that; I felt supported.

But that isn't always the case. Sometimes enacting your treatment plan and surrendering to the wave of sorrow will have you breaking down alone, but in a public place. I've done this plenty of times. It seems my preferred location for a solo breakdown when away from home is the bathroom. On multiple occasions through the years, I have escaped to a public restroom to let the tears flow. I've done this at Chick-fil-A, P.F. Chang's, and the American Airlines Center in Dallas, TX before the start of a Beyoncé concert. (I did it, I got Beyoncé in my book.)

And then there are the times when you break down around strangers. For me, one of those was in 2014 at a dentist's office in Denton, TX. I was in the chair waiting for the dentist and looked up at the monitor that held my information to find a picture of me—pregnant with Chase—on the screen. I didn't even have time to make it to the bathroom. I just cried in the chair and used the plastic bib someone had clipped around my neck as a napkin. Someone awkwardly approached me to ask if I needed anything, and I just told them I was going to need a new bib.

This kind of behavior is very off-brand for the pre-March 23, 2013 version of me but very on-brand for who I am now. The old version of me wasn't a crier; the new version of me very much is. The old version of me was an unhealthy Achiever—focused primarily on productivity, accomplishing things, and checking stuff off the to-do list. Don't get me wrong, I still enjoy checking things off the to-do list, but this is no longer primary. Achievement is no longer the driver of my day. I have learned to be OK with items left unchecked on my to-do list. I have greater needs than a clean kitchen.

I need healing, rest, and restoration. That was true ten years ago, and it is still true now—and I choose to practice my treatment plan daily to help me incrementally experience them more.

→ What's your response?

Griefs and Sorrows

Gentle Reminder

You are not lazy; you're grieving.
Rest is healing.
Being vulnerable feels like weakness,
but it is a display of strength.

Meditation

Consider what items would serve you well in
your treatment plan or care package.
A few questions to consider:
What small things bring you joy? (i.e., Opening
the blinds, listening to a favorite song, lighting
a candle, etc.)
Is creating more space on your calendar for rest
an option? If so, make adjustments as necessary.
What is one way you can care for your body during
this time? (I.e., drink more water, go for a walk, eat more
nutrients, create a sleep routine, practice deep breathing)

The Shouts of God

Excerpt from a blog post dated January 14, 2014,

*"The abundance of God's revelation is
usually accompanied by a thorn in the flesh"*
(2 Corinthians 12:7).
C.H. Spurgeon, Beside Still Waters[5]

*"We can ignore even pleasure. But pain insists upon being
attended to. God whispers to us in our pleasures, speaks in
our conscience, but shouts in our pains: it is his megaphone
to rouse a deaf world."*
C.S. Lewis, The Problem of Pain[6]

*In April, a friend recommended that I subscribe
to daily emails from a ministry called GriefShare.
These emails have been such a huge encouragement—
speaking some very hard truths at just the right time.
For more information about this ministry or to subscribe
to the emails, visit www.GriefShare.org.*

*This is a piece of the message from Day 283
that I had in my inbox today:*

*When logic doesn't seem to apply and being in
control is not an option, you are left feeling*

vulnerable. This is the point at which you are ready to learn. Recognize the need to learn more about God in order to live.
"He learned obedience from what he suffered" (Hebrews 5:8).
Father God, I am ready to listen and learn from You. Help me to be still before You in worshipful silence. Amen[7]

This is so true. In grief, the Lord has revealed Himself to me like never before. Like the C.S. Lewis quote, it's like He is shouting. Shouting truths I thought I understood but didn't. Truths like,
He loves me.
He is good and does good.

(7)

The What If? Game

Practice Presence: *Take a moment of stillness to breathe deeply to prepare yourself to be present with my words and your reactions and responses. (See Appendix B for suggested breath practices.)*

I don't know about you, but I tend to overthink. It is easy for me to get lost in my world of thoughts. Sometimes that looks like obsessively recounting what a situation could have gone like:

What else could I have said?

What did I communicate with my facial expressions and body language?

What do they think of me now as a result of the conversation?

Are they mad at me?

Do they like me?

Will they want to hang out with me again?

Other times the energy is spent weighing possible scenarios of a particular situation.

If I put the boys in school, what will our new schedule be?

Will the other homeschool moms judge me?

Have I failed?

Will I be able to adjust to the schedule?

How will we manage homework and school activities?

What are the pros of homeschooling?

What are the cons?
What are the pros of putting the boys in school?
What are the cons?

You could refer to this mental activity as discursive reasoning, worrying, or maybe just excessive thinking. In the Buddhist tradition, this obsessive activity of the thinking mind is referred to as the "monkey mind," which refers to a mind that is unsettled, restless, or confused. I prided myself in my ability to have my thinking mind constantly churning. It was as if I needed my busy mind to validate my experience, identity, or existence. As Descartes's quote goes, "I think therefore I am."[8]

If this is my tendency in calm seasons of life, it definitely became amplified in grief. My thinking mind went into a hyperactive mode, I believe in an attempt to try and make sense of what I was experiencing.

Why did this happen to me?
What did I do wrong?
Is God judging me?
Why is God judging me?
How come there are not many people around me who have experienced this?
What could I have done to make the outcome different?
Was it because I didn't breastfeed until he was 12 months of age?
Was it because I had Group B strep?
Did I not feed him a good enough diet?
Did I not do enough things to help his immune system be strong?
What if I had gone into the room earlier?
What if we had gone to a different hospital?
What if we had different doctors?
What if I would not have had two miscarriages before I got pregnant with him?

My mind was like a snowball rolling down a hill—it was picking up mass and speed, and I did not know how to stop it. Though I didn't enjoy playing, my mind seemed to especially love what I call the What If? game. This game brought me great pain, but my mind would play it by default. One quote that eventually became a huge help was from Corrie Ten Boom's book *The Hiding Place*. I had read the book one month before Chase passed, and I was struck by something she said as she recounted her and her sister's experience of being trapped in a concentration camp. Struggling with the brutality of what they were facing, she says, "There are no what ifs in the will of God."[9]

Thank you, Mind. I'm actually grateful you retained and recalled this quote. It immediately became an anchor. When my mind began to drift toward the What If? game, I'd call this anchor to mind, and it would calm my thoughts and redirect them to the truth that God was in control. Even though I didn't understand it, it would bring with it a momentary calm.

This was probably the first intentional mindset work I did in grief. But unfortunately, this alone wasn't enough.

Not only did I have lots of questions, but my mental chatter also continued with its own narratives and conclusions.

I am being punished.

I did something wrong.

That is why my son died, because of my sin.

I did something to deserve this.

This will never end. I will never make it.

One day I found myself in a conversation with a friend, and I casually shared some of these conclusions. I saw no problem with them, but her first response was, that's not how God's voice sounds. At that moment, I felt hopeless and paralyzed.

Well, what does God's voice sound like, then?

I guess I can't trust myself to discern what God's voice sounds like.

I knew the Scriptures encouraged us to set our minds on things above and to take every thought captive to Christ. I also knew the mind was a battlefield, and the enemy could easily sway me through lies and half-truths. I guess it was time to add mindset work to my treatment plan.

Oh Lord, this is exhausting.

I just want to be left alone and be sad.

Oh, I'm easy prey for the enemy?

The enemy doesn't take it easy on grieving moms?

I have to fight?

Yes, I chose to fight. Again, primarily for the sake of the child growing in my womb. I began by trying to intentionally choose where I would set my mind and what stories I would believe. But as mentioned before, I didn't trust my ability to always land on the truth. So I enlisted help from others and began practicing what I called "thought vomiting."

I'll admit this is kind of a gross picture, but that is what it felt like. Whatever thoughts came across my mind, I would find a trusted friend or family member and share all the noise in my head. Thankfully, I had kind and thoughtful listeners to support me in this process. If and when I said something inaccurate, something that did not align with how God's voice sounds, they would gently offer me a new narrative, a new story to tell myself, or a new conclusion to land on. It was not always easy to practice believing what they said. Many times it felt wrong, uncomfortable, and untrue. But I chose to trust their wisdom over my own.

A beautiful illustration of the work I'm encouraging can be found in the Marvel film *Doctor Strange in the Multiverse of Madness*. Driven by deep anger and sadness, Scarlet Witch attacks Kamartaj, a training ground where sorcerers learn techniques to defend Earth against mystic threats. As the warrior sorcerers of Kamartaj face the very real and present threat of Scarlet Witch, who has the power to get inside their minds and deceive them with spells, Sorcerer Supreme Wong yells a warning to his warriors, "Fortify your minds!"[10] Wong knew Scarlet Witch had paused to find an individual she could easily manipulate with her telepathic powers, and he was commanding them to guard against it.

I still struggle with the "monkey mind," and at times, I find myself in the beginning phases of the What If? game. But after ten years of practice to guard my thoughts and pursue peace by keeping my mind fixed on God (Isaiah 26:3), I can tell my mind is more fortified, and I have experienced more joy because of it.

→ What's your response?

Gentle Reminder

"There are no "what ifs" in the will of God."

Meditation

Take a few minutes to allow mental chatter about your day or your loss. Write down some of the stories you are telling yourself. If you are willing to adopt any new narratives, write them down.
As you end your time, make a promise to use the new narratives as a way to "talk back" to the old ones.

Interlude - Sound Healing

Listen to the song "Though You Slay Me" by Lauren Chandler or Shane & Shane. Take a moment to note anything that stood out during your listening. (See Appendix A for helpful postures you can take while listening.)

The Ugly Truth

A blog post from August 3, 2013,

For some reason in a season of grief, you get a free pass to act and think how you want. I lost my son, so I don't have to care about you or your story—kind of thinking.

The ugly truth is my heart is not perfect. It wants to turn its nose up at the pain of others. It wants to elevate itself. It wants to invalidate their pain.

The ugly truth is my initial heart response to hearing a radio ad about a mom whose son was paralyzed by a texting driver was, "Who cares? You can still talk to and play with your son."

The ugly truth is I sometimes look at the success of others and think, "Oh good, you get a promotion. I get to mourn the loss of my baby."

I am not going to be perfect in this season—can't be.

But the good news, in the midst of my ugly truths, God's grace is still sufficient. Grace covers my sin. Grace forgives. Grace enables me to confess and repent—often.

8

Blasphemy

Practice Presence: Take a moment of stillness to breathe deeply to prepare yourself to be present with my words and your reactions and responses. (See Appendix B for suggested breath practices.)

It's not uncommon to think, say, and do some wild things in grief. You will probably even surprise yourself with the depths you can sink to, but I believe part of fighting for joy is telling the truth—being honest about what's happening and what you're feeling. As Dr. Angela Gorrell says in her book, *The Gravity of Joy*, "Joy is not naïve."[11] Even though people may be afraid and unable to handle our truths, that is not true of God. God can meet us in the depths. God can handle all of our questions. God can handle all of our thoughts. God knows them already and is not surprised. God welcomes us to approach the throne anyway, despite the wild things that may come to our minds.

In addition, I believe we need the same support from people when we are grieving. It's nice to feel we can be honest with those in our trusted circle about the severity of our pain. I needed the freedom to fully express what I was feeling without the fear of being judged. I longed for people who could hold space for me and with me—people who would witness and acknowledge rather than judge and correct. I needed people who could validate my frustration rather than be afraid of it. I needed permission to be human. The human experience can be messy and complex, and I understand and appreciate this way more than I did ten years ago.

I grew up in a Western American church culture. When I say Western, I am not referring to the Western part of the United States, I'm referring to the modern use of the words West or Western to refer to areas of the world primarily of European origin. Areas like the United States, Canada, the European Union, Australia and New Zealand. I intentionally call out my Western roots to contrast them against characteristics common in Indigenous and Eastern cultures. Western values prioritize the destination over the journey, the answer over the question. Eastern values prioritize the journey, the learning process itself. As such, sojourners are given freedom and encouragement to ask questions. The church culture I grew up in taught me I needed to believe the "right" things, do the "right" things, and speak the "right" things. I was meant to comply—no questions asked.

And who defined what was "right?" They did. Looking back, I can see that their definition of "right" left no room for questions, struggle, doubt, hurt, or the rawness of human emotion and experience. In that setting, not only were these things unwelcome, they were deemed as "bad." This Western way heavily influenced my life. I was someone always aiming and striving for "right." I had to be right and do right and think right. But after losing a child, it was hard to find right in something that felt wrong.

I slowly began to give myself permission to feel, think, and do things that didn't align with the narrow definition of "right" I had been given. Over the last decade, I have questioned and wrestled with many things I was taught—especially in church spaces. Many from my past would describe these thoughts, and maybe even the sheer act of questioning, as blasphemous. The Oxford Dictionary defines blasphemy as "the act or offense of speaking sacrilegiously about God or sacred things; profane talk."

In my experience, having blasphemous thoughts in grief is not uncommon. I've already mentioned there were moments when God felt cruel like he was punishing me. I also found myself forming blasphemous thoughts against God's people, who are sacred because they are made in God's image.

An individual tried to appease my pain not even a month after Chase passed, offering, "Well, you don't even know how many people will be impacted by your story. There will be people that come to know the Lord as a result of you losing Chase." In response, I thought to myself, *Screw those people; they can burn in hell. I want my son back.*

I don't feel that way now, but it was where I was at the moment. Tedashii shared a similar sentiment, and our friends around us gave us space to be in it. It's almost as if they understood in grief, that a lot of words would be thrown around, but many of them would be like dust in the wind—they'll float away rather than take up permanent residence. We needed this unspoken permission from them to share our ugly truths. I see it now as a gift from some in our community —they made space for us to practice vulnerability and, in doing so, helped to disallow shame in our lives.

When we exist in communities where we feel we must always say and do the right things, it can be a breeding ground for shame. In this environment, a culture has not been set for honesty and vulnerability, so rather than being free to share the thoughts I am struggling with, I hold them within. As a result, the thoughts continue to haunt me. Oftentimes, we begin descending into a shame spiral, and it can be hard to get off and find higher ground. Here's what my shame spiral looks like in response to thinking a negative thought: *Woah, where did that come from? Oh no, it's not OK to think this. I am a terrible person. I know I am not supposed to do this. What would my friends say if they found out? I bet God is mad at me now. I can't share this with anyone; they would never accept me.* And on and on we go.

When I am free to bring my inner thoughts to the light in the presence of another image-bearer and still be loved and accepted, they become an embodied representation of God's love and acceptance. The listener's love and acceptance in response to my shameful thinking helps push shame away. It's like Dr. Curt Thompson, psychiatrist, speaker, and author of *The Soul of Shame: Retelling the Stories We Believe About Ourselves*, says, "Shame always requires outside help for healing. My shame needs you."[12] But you can't help my shame heal if you don't make space for me to share openly.

Our thoughts are unpredictable. They will come and go. It's highly likely you have had or will have some streams of blasphemous thoughts on this grief journey. It's not every thought I am concerned with. It's the ones that become stories, the ones we attach to, I'm most concerned about. Please permit yourself to be honest about your blasphemous thoughts. Then, I hope you will let them move, and you will land on and hold on to only true thoughts.

→ What's your response?

Blasphemy

Gentle Reminder

You are not your thoughts.

Meditation

Imagine what it would look and feel like to exist in a community that disallowed shame. What is one thing you can do to help make this a reality?

The Natural Order

Excerpts from a journal entry dated April 8, 2013,

There is a "natural order" in life we think our lives should follow. It says we should live to an old age, and the older sibling should do everything first—graduate college, get married, and have kids. It also says a parent, the one who is there on the day of their child's birth, should never be there on the day of their death.

But God is not bound by this natural order. He created natural laws but exists outside of them. By his sovereignty, the sun can stand still, donkeys can talk, bodies of water can become walls, the dead can be raised, and the lame can walk. None of these things could be if God was bound by the "natural order."

9

Nature's Remedy

Therefore let those who suffer according to God's will entrust their souls to a faithful Creator while doing good.
1 Peter 4:19, ESV

The heavens declare the glory of God, and the sky above proclaims his handiwork.
Psalm 19:1, ESV

Practice Presence: *Take a moment of stillness to breathe deeply to prepare yourself to be present with my words and your reactions and responses. (See Appendix B for suggested breath practices.)*

The opening journal entry shared some of my frustration with how we use the phrase "natural order" in our culture. It usually centers more on what humans decide is the right way to live. But there is a natural order I enjoy—and that's the natural order existing in nature. Nature has been restoring and healing for me over the last decade.

The scriptures listed above are two that caught my eye back in April 2013 and have had a lasting impression on me ever since. In reading 1 Peter 4:18, I was kind of shocked Peter referenced the fact that God is Creator in the verse. I'm not sure what I expected to see there instead, but I was unable to move quickly past that word. So I began to ponder what it meant to entrust my soul to a faithful Creator, and I soon found myself thinking about the beauty and wonder of creation.

This led me to read the creation account in Genesis 1 and 2. As I read, a question from a Bible study I had done years prior resurfaced—"What kind of God creates like this?" Then I was reminded of these beautiful characteristics of our Creator—intentional, creative, One who brings order to chaos, intimately involved in the details, the Creator and modeler of rest, all-powerful, all-sustaining, good.

After that, I admired nature more; it was just raw creation. Mankind's hand was absent from making it beautiful. Instead, it was God's words of wisdom alone that had spoken it into being, and God's loving oversight that had sustained it. Nature helps me better understand how big my God is.

Tedashii, Jaden, and I visited the Grand Canyon a month after losing Chase. All I could do was stare in awe. I remember feeling a sense of peace because the Creator of this masterpiece was watching over me—and watching over Chase. There were several other lessons I learned on the train ride to the Grand Canyon. Here's an excerpt from a journal entry dated April 7, 2013.

"Blessed are those whose strength is in you, in whose heart are the highways to Zion. As they go through the valley of Baca, they make it a place of springs; the early rain also covers it with pools."
Psalm 84:5-6, ESV

Riding on the train to the Grand Canyon—very much in the valley . . . It is dry, desolate, uneven, and low. There are rocks and brush, dirt, and more rocks. The valley is long, and it is wide. There are a few animals, not much stuff that would sustain life. But the valley doesn't go on forever. In the distance, you can see mountains. And we ourselves are headed to a gorgeous, breathtaking destination, the Grand Canyon. There are no homes in this valley, no places for shelter, for comfort. There are a few cows roaming about, but not many. It seems that no one lives in this valley. To my left and my right, there are no homes. The people in the valley are us—the people on the train. The ground is cracked. Dry. There are some places where you can't see the mountains in the distance, but you know they are there.

Observations of the text:

- "Blessed are those whose strength is in You"—not in themselves, or in a friend, but in You.
- "in whose heart are the highways to Zion"—their hearts are hopeful.
- "as they go"—we all must go through the valley of weeping (the school of suffering).
- "go through"—we don't stay in the valley, we go through it; practically, our season of weeping will come to an end.
- "they make it"—I have a choice! What will I make of the situation? I can choose to listen to my flesh, the enemy, the world, or I can trust in God and believe His truth.
- "a place of springs"—something you never find in this valley. The very thought sounds crazy to the outside world; springs plural →, abundant, flourishing, a place that can sustain life.
- "the early rains"—Do you begin to see things differently after choosing to focus on Him who brings joy? Maybe you can now view things in such a way that

they promote you to life, not death.

Once we reached the Grand Canyon, I stared in awe and thought to myself, Chase is with the Creator of this; he's OK.

A few weeks after this trip, we visited Florida. I went on prayer walks up and down the beach and just couldn't take my eyes off the water. I couldn't see where it stopped, and it was breathtaking. The Creator of this magnificent view was asking me to entrust myself to Him. My beach-inspired prayer became: *Lord, help me go willingly where You're leading, even if I can't see the destination.*

Fast forward to a cool morning in October, and I found myself on a mini-hike near Branson, MO. I was speechless as I witnessed the changing colors of the lake, the sky, and the autumn-colored trees as the sun rose higher and higher in the sky. I thanked God I had the chance to behold such beauty on this earth. And, once again, I felt excited, looking forward to the reunion I would have with Chase in the New Heavens and the New Earth. Looking forward to beholding beauty there far outweighs anything I have or will ever see here. I speak of the beauty of the Lord, of course, but also the indescribable beauty of the New Earth— the renewed creation.

Each of these trips was bittersweet, painful, refreshing, agonizing, relaxing, and healing.

Spending time in nature has been a consistent practice over this decade. There is a peace and calm I experience when I find stillness in nature. It is a chance to learn wisdom and commune with God. I have learned a lot of science to explain the benefits to our mind and body of various nature-based practices: grounding (standing barefoot on the earth), forest bathing, sunbathing, desert bathing, and taking in the fresh air. But I don't need books and articles to tell me that being in nature always makes me feel just a little bit better. There's something life-giving about creation. Maybe because the Creator is the ultimate Life-giver.

→ What's your response?

Gentle Reminder

You can practice the presence of God by spending time in nature. Solomon learned wisdom from nature—you can too.

Meditation - Nature Practice

Spend 5 to 10 minutes sitting still in nature, reminding yourself that the Creator is present with you now. If it feels right for you, sit on the ground or allow your bare feet to make contact with the earth.

The Shadow and the Form

A blog post from July 20, 2013,

"We tend to start with Earth and reason up towards Heaven when instead we should start with Heaven and reason down towards Earth. It isn't merely an accommodation to our earthly familial structure, for instance, that God calls Himself a father and us children. On the contrary, he created father-child relationships to display his relationships with us."
-- Randy Alcorn, Heaven[13]

I have been encouraged recently by dwelling on this idea. The idea is that Earth is not the starting point of all things, but rather an extension of something greater. It makes most sense in my head to think about Earth as the shadow of a beautiful form, the form being Heaven, and all that exists there.

Honestly, I have never given much thought to Heaven until this season of grief began. Until I had a deep, intimate, and personal relationship with a person who, without warning, suddenly ended up there. And not just any human, a boy, that I birthed—my son.

But in missing Chase, I do not grieve like those who have no hope. I grieve with hope (1 Thessalonians 4:13). And recently, it's been the hope of Heaven that allows my tears to eventually stop.

The hope of Heaven reminds me Chase is safe. He is in a place free of sin and suffering. He is happy. He has a never-ending, unable-to-be-stolen joy. That brings me great comfort. As I experience joy and happiness here, I can't help but to think Chase is experiencing it in a more full, more intensified manner. The same way our experience is magnified when we interact with the true form of something, rather than its shadow.

(10)

Triumphant Heart

Practice Presence: *Take a moment of stillness to breathe deeply to prepare yourself to be present with my words and your reactions and responses. (See Appendix B for suggested breath practices.)*

I don't know where I would be without hope. Early on, my primary anchors were the truths that God is good and God is in control. By faith, hope is an anchor. Hebrews 11:1, NIV says, "Now faith is confidence in what we hope for and assurance about what we do not see."

A common scripture read in times of pain comes from 2 Corinthians 4:8-9, NIV. I quoted from it earlier in this book, but let me do it again.

"We are hard pressed on every side, but not crushed; perplexed, but not in despair; persecuted, but not abandoned; struck down, but not destroyed."

This scripture gave me permission. It permitted me to be perplexed. I was confused. I did not understand, and as much as I wanted a succinct phrase explaining why I had to go through this experience, I knew I would not get it. It was too complex to be boiled down into a simple statement. This scripture also gave me boundaries – through the power and protection of the Holy Spirit, it kept me from despair.

At times when I believed the pain would never end, I would never survive, and there was no point in living, a quiet voice within would remind me that God was there, I wasn't alone, and I had a reason to hope. Not only was God with me, but this scripture in 1 Peter 5:8-9, NIV, which I had been studying before grief, reminded me that others were with me too.

"Be alert and of sober mind. Your enemy the devil prowls around like a roaring lion looking for someone to devour. Resist him, standing firm in the faith, because you know that the family of believers throughout the world is undergoing the same kind of sufferings."

These words were a balm to my soul. Though I had met with two moms who had similar stories, I couldn't point to anyone else in my current (close or extended) circle who knew the loss of a child. When I read this scripture, it moved me to expand my scope. I began to consider people around my city, state, nation, world, and those who existed before me. I was reminded I was not the only person in history to know the pain of losing a child, and that was strangely comforting. I admit I did play the comparative suffering game for a moment, but I took no joy in the pain of others. Nevertheless, I was grateful I had examples to look at, examples that showed me survival was possible after losing a child.

This pondering moved me to become a more empathetic person. I read the book, *From Grief to Glory* by James W. Bruce, which recounts the stories of numerous parents of the 18th and 19th centuries who knew about the loss of a child. I instantly connected to their stories and expressed empathy. Some of the parents lost multiple babies, others lost older children. There was comfort in knowing there were others who knew these horrors, and they were not crushed under the weight of the unimaginable.

The day after Chase passed, a friend picked me up from my house to take me to meet with a mom who knew this pain.

She didn't talk much, and I appreciated that. She offered me a smoothie from Jamba Juice and said something along the lines of, "I don't have words, but I will just give you this. Psalm 34:18, says the Lord is near to the brokenhearted and saves the crushed in spirit." In hindsight, at that moment, I believe she planted a seed that would bear the fruit of my holding on to hope.

I think the act of holding on to hope is an act of joy. Holding on to hope means actively rejecting despair. Last year, I heard a quote that perfectly captures this idea. "I look at joy as an act of resistance against despair and all its forces."[14] Let's visit the Oxford Dictionary one more time. Despair is defined as the complete loss or absence of hope.

Yes, yes, yes! My choice to fight for joy and hold onto hope was simultaneously an act of resistance against despair. Hope and joy are available because of the truth of Emmanuel—God with us. This fuels my triumphant heart. God is with me. I need to remember this—in every moment of every day. This probably explains why I'm passionate about practicing the presence of God: in nature, on the mat, in arguments, in games with the boys, at rest time, when I enjoy good ice cream, when stuck in Atlanta traffic . . . you get the idea.

I don't understand why loss is part of my story, but I know it is not arbitrary or meaningless; I know God has a purpose in it. I believed, most of the time, that God loved me, but it was hard to accept God's love was present when Chase took his last breath. It was hard to accept this nightmare we found ourselves in had been filtered through His hand of love before He allowed it to touch us. Frustrating. Mind-blowing. But I choose to keep going, living in the truth that, though my heart is bleeding, it is also triumphant because God loves me and is with me always.

→ What's your response?

Gentle Reminder

*Even though it may feel like it—you are not alone.
"Joy is an act of resistance against despair."*

Meditation

*What is the tangible hope you will hold on to? List
some reasons why you will fight for joy and
actively resist despair.*

Interlude - Sound Healing

*Listen to the song "Moving Forward" by Israel
Houghton. Take a moment to note anything that
stood out during your listening.
(See Appendix A for helpful postures you
can take while listening.)*

The Little While

A blog post from October 17, 2013,

*And after you have suffered a little while, the God of all
grace, who has called you to his eternal glory in Christ, will
himself restore, confirm, strengthen and establish you.*
1 Peter 5:10, ESV

*...but we rejoice in our sufferings, knowing that suffering
produces endurance, and endurance produces character,
and character produces hope, and hope does not put us to
shame, because God's love has been poured into our hearts
through the Holy Spirit who has been given to us.*
Romans 5:3-5, ESV

*After a hard day, I went to bed begging for the strength and
endurance needed to endure the "little while." I don't know
what my "little while" is. Is it this very intense season of
grief? Is it the time I have left here on Earth? Either way,
in the grand scale of eternity, it truly is a little while.*

*Not only is the idea of it being a "little while" comforting
but I'm also moved to thanksgiving when I think about
the promises given in the 1 Peter verse above.*

The God of all grace will restore me.

JOY IN THE MOURNING

The God of all grace will confirm me.
The God of all grace will strengthen me.
The God of all grace will establish me.

God has not left me, and He never will. The God of
all-sufficient grace is providing hope, endurance,
strength, and restoration.

I've never been more thankful for the Lord's promises
of peace and comfort and joy and abundant life than I
am right now. Because I see now that, in the depths of
despair, this is what my heart longs for. It doesn't long for
money, a particular dress size or number on the scale,
or a problem-free life; these items are not warm blankets
to the soul. But God's promises are.

I'm confident God is good and faithful—He always
keeps His word. Therefore, I have an unshakeable
confidence that I will make it through my "little while."

(11)

One Moment at A Time

*So we do not lose heart. Though our outer self is
wasting away, our inner self is being renewed day by
day. For this light momentary affliction is preparing for
us an eternal weight of glory beyond all comparison, as
we look not to the things that are seen but to the things
that are unseen. For the things that are seen are
transient, but the things that are unseen are eternal.*
2 Corinthians 4:16-18, ESV

Whew. My God. I never thought I'd make it.

It's Sunday morning, March 24, 2013, and I sat on a brown
couch listening to another mom and dad share their story of
losing their son three years earlier. No way. There was no way
I would make it three years. No part of me could fathom even
making it three weeks. I knew I wouldn't be able to handle the
pain and the sadness. Yet here I am—10 years later. That is
nothing but the grace of God.

At the beginning of this journey, looking far down the
timeline seemed incomprehensible. Something that did seem
feasible was focusing on each moment, and I was reminded
that God's mercies were there. Lamentations 3:22-23, ESV
says, "The steadfast love of the Lord never ceases; his mercies
never come to an end; they are new every morning; great is
your faithfulness." I understood mercies to mean help, so now,
when I felt helpless, I could tell myself that help was available.

At the end of the day, I would go to bed convinced there would be new mercies tomorrow. When tomorrow came, I believed the new mercies were there and resolved to exhaust them. This was my day-by-day rhythm. But before it became a day-by-day rhythm, it was my moment-by-moment rhythm—exhausting the new mercies, leaning into waves of sorrow, and being present with my pain.

In those early moments and days, the scripture above from 2 Corinthians was offensive. Nothing about my experience felt light and momentary. It was heavy and never-ending. Over time, I began to believe my pain, especially the excruciating nature of it, would end; though I did not know when. And the thought of pain coming to an end sent my mind to remember my experiences in labor, with both Jaden and Chase.

My labors and births were not excruciating, but there was definitely discomfort. My midwife, Jean, helped me prepare for them by reminding me that contractions were like waves, they came and went, and they were not constant in duration. They had a rise and fall; they were not constant in intensity. She encouraged me to take it one wave at a time, and now, as a doula, I tell my clients the same. In labor, part of my work is to stay present with each wave, and to ride it, surrender to it, rather than resist it. And I have done this, over and over, for hours in labor. In my labors, and those of others I have supported, it is not uncommon for mom's eyes to regularly drift towards the clock, silently thinking to herself, *How much longer? How much more?*

Those questions are not easily answered in labor; no one knows exactly how much longer it will be until the baby is welcomed to the earthside. We just commit to taking each wave one at a time, knowing that at some point, labor does come to an end—this baby will not be in my body forever. That's kind of how my life is now. I often ask the question *How long, O Lord?* And I never get an answer. I just keep going. And I have decided that my keeping going is a way to honor Chase.

I even had to be very mindful and conscious of the words I use to refer to my keeping going on this path. Some people have a philosophy that I need to "get over it." I think that's ridiculous, and I want to urge them to stop saying this to people. There is no getting over the loss of a child. Others carry the philosophy to "move on." I cringe less at this idea, but even it left me with a bad taste in my mouth—because for me, "moving on" came with a connotation of leaving behind, and no part of me is willing to leave Chase behind. So I concluded I would move forward. One moment at a time, one day at a time, knowing my story has a good ending.

As it's been said before, this journey can be complex and unpredictable. When the storm first hit, the weight seemed too heavy to bear. I can attest to the truth that the intensity of the pain has lightened, but I still have to leave room for those times when the pain hits like a violent wave. This roller coaster lifestyle is just something I've become accustomed to. There are days when I feel steady and incredibly confident in God's love, and then there are days when I find myself doubting it. There are days when I am eager to draw closer to God, and there are days when I feel like I kind of don't want to have anything to do with Him. Sometimes I feel like a confused, sad, and angry little girl beating on her father's chest as he holds her in his lap. *Ugh, I'm so mad at you! But I know you love me, and I don't have anywhere else to go.* Sometimes it feels like a trap. But it's a confusing trap because love and new mercies are there. Joy is there. Comfort is there.

I want to be honest, I'm not "OK," things are not "OK." I miss Chase every day. I miss him on Mother's Day, Father's Day, Christmas, and New Year's. I miss him on his birthday, Jaden's birthday, Callen's birthday, and Kai's birthday. I miss him on what could have been his first day of preschool, kindergarten, first grade, second grade, third grade, fourth grade, and fifth grade. I miss him when I miss him. There's a quote I often use in fitness classes or labor readiness conversations with my doula clients, "A comfort zone is a beautiful place, but nothing ever grows there."[15] The encouragement that follows is this— get comfortable with being uncomfortable. That's what I have decided to do.

I'm not "OK." This is uncomfortable, but I know I have been and am continuing to be mended and healed. The journey of grief and restoration is long, and I choose to move forward with a hopeful expectancy for the day when my healing is complete.

→ What's your response?

Gentle Reminder

In every moment, there are new mercies available to you.

Meditation

In the movie The Shack, God is personified as a mother, played by Octavia Spencer, for the majority of the film. During a pivotal scene when the main character has to go do the unimaginable, bury his child, as he heads out, he realizes Octavia is not going with him. He questions her, and she responds, "You're going to need a Father for this."[16]

How do you need God to show up for you right now as you prepare to take your next forward steps on this path? Do you need a mother figure, a father figure, a loving friend, or maybe just embodied comfort? Visualize and allow yourself to experience God, who is showing up exactly as you need.

Death Has Died

Blog post dated September 13, 2013,

Music has been such a huge part of my restoration process. Listen to the song "Death Has Died" by Andy Mineo. It celebrates the truth that one day there will be no more death. We still live in a broken world, a world with sin, suffering, disease, disaster, despair—and death.

But there is a day coming when Christ will return, and all will be made new. Things that seem sad will turn out to be untrue. Tears of pain and sadness will be no more —God will wipe them all away.

Not only has it been so healing for me, but since Jaden is such a fan of hip-hop, especially all things Reach Records, it has allowed us to have some beautiful conversations. He listens intently to the lyrics and then asks me questions:

"Andy said his Grandma died. Just like Chasey died?"

"God is going to one day wipe away every tear from my eyes?"

We discuss topics I never thought I'd talk about with my 3-year-old, but I'm praying the Lord would allow the seeds planted to blossom into truths Jaden embraces and believes, truths that he'll anchor his life on.

I know a better day is coming. The Apostle Paul says in 1 Corinthians 15:19, ESV, "If in Christ we have hope in this life only, we are of all people most to be pitied." But he goes on to explain that Christ has in fact raised from the dead! And those in Him have an amazing future hope! A hope that includes forever life and the destruction of every enemy! The last enemy to be destroyed is death! (1 Corinthians 15:26)

Yes!

PART 3

A Guide

Interlude - Sound Healing

Listen to the song "In Christ Alone", lyrics by Keith Getty and Stuart Townend. Take a moment to note anything that stands out during your listening. (See Appendix A for helpful postures you can take while listening.)

12

A Theology of Praise and Lament

I don't know about you, but at the beginning of grief, I realized I needed a new theology of praise and lament, celebration and suffering. In his book, *Prophetic Lament*, Dr. Soong-Chan Rah helped expose this reality even more and gave me words to rebuild a more robust theology. To this day, this book is probably the most instrumental in my grief journey. Let me take a moment to borrow from the wise words of Dr. Rah.

He explains we live in a culture of victory and triumph; as a result, we have become accustomed to winning and things going our way. We're not accustomed to loss. He explains how this phenomenon shows up in our worship music, citing that about 90% of the songs we sing when we gather in our respective church assemblies are celebratory. Nothing may seem inherently disturbing with this number until he reveals that 40% of the Psalms are lament or sorrowful in nature.

I agree with his premise that this over-focus on praise has made us forget the reality of suffering. He defines celebration as the language of praise and lament as the language of suffering. Here are a few quotes to help us grow a more complete understanding of lament.

"Lament stems from an acute experience of pain . . . It is the human response to pain and adversity, and is not bound by the rules of praise . . . Lament is an act of protest as the lamenter is allowed to express indignation and even outrage about the experience of suffering . . .

The one who laments can call out to God for help, and in that outcry there is the hope and even the manifestation of praise."[17]

I'll say it again, we need a theology of praise and lament, celebration and suffering—not just one or the other.

Let me take this one step further.

Theology is what we know about God. Spirituality is what we can experience of God. My hope is that a more robust theology of praise and lament will lead us to deeper experiences of God.

In our Western, black-and-white, binary culture, we can benefit from what I have heard many call "the power of and." There must be room for celebration AND lament. Joy AND sorrow. Suffering AND liberation. Struggle AND belief.

As I have put on these new lenses, I can more clearly see how this often doesn't exist in church spaces. I have observed countless examples of people recounting difficult experiences they are going through.

My son is addicted to drugs . . .

My spouse cheated on me . . .

My work environment is toxic, and as a result, I am suffering from severe anxiety . . .

Can you guess the words that follow the comma in the above phrases? "But I'm still trusting God." It's almost as if we use the phrase as a way to minimize the significance of the hardship. I am a fan of the full stop.

My work environment is toxic. (full stop)

My spouse cheated on me. (full stop)

My work environment is toxic and as a result, I am suffering from severe anxiety. (full stop)

Period. Full stop. We don't need a "but" statement to follow. In grammar, "but" often erases what came before it. I am not in the business of erasing the hardship and pain and struggle of others. We can do ourselves a service by incorporating the power of "and." Let's adopt "and" rather than "but" . . .

My son is struggling with drugs, and I still trust the Lord.

This is the kind of God we serve anyway, a God of superabundance who has more than enough room for our pain AND our praises. This is the type of robust theology we need to serve us well in life, not only in times of suffering.

I admit that before loss I had not spent much time contemplating the truth of Heaven. But now that our son was there, we wanted to know more. Initially, Jesus seemed a consolation prize. It was nice He was there, but we longed for Heaven because of Chase. Eventually, my desire for Heaven grew to be motivated by a longing for the Savior, and as that grew, I gained new lenses to see my present reality more clearly—we live in a fallen world. Brokenness, pain, and sadness abound here because of sin. Somehow, I'd forgotten. I was a walking example of Soong-Chan Rah's point, a theology with an "absence of suffering doesn't make the heart grow fonder; it makes the heart forget."[18]

I had allowed myself to be lulled to sleep by the reality of pain and suffering. I saw them as unwanted interruptions to the normal "business as usual" life of ease and comfort. The more my vision became less blurred, the more I realized pain and suffering were the norms in a fallen world. Ease and comfort became the welcomed interruptions. I began to read scripture with new eyes and suddenly found the Bible screaming with the realities of a faithful God who not only has a purpose within the pain but is a constant presence to those suffering.

The main encouragement of this chapter is this: anchor in the word.

An obvious source to help us develop this robust theology is the Scriptures. There are plenty of examples in the scriptures of celebration and sorrow, so read them and let yourself sit in the reality of the tension. Celebrate the fact that God rescued Noah and his family in the ark and lament that the rest of humanity, those not walking with God, were washed away in the flood. Celebrate Israel's liberation from slavery in Egypt, and hold the heaviness of Egypt's loss of all its firstborns. Celebrate Christ's resurrection on the third day, and hold the weight of the sadness his family and disciples endured when he died on Friday.

Throughout the scriptures, there are numerous examples where both celebration and suffering are possible, as well as stories that go unresolved. Ugh, this can be frustrating! We don't always get a nice summary of what happens next; we don't get the concluding statement, "And they lived happily ever after." We are left with questions. The same is true in grief. I have questions. I am living on this side. The story is unresolved. And I have to live in that. It's annoying at times and uncomfortable, but as I've mentioned before, I have learned to get comfortable with being uncomfortable.

To all my musicians, I'm sure you can understand and appreciate this example. Have you ever heard a musical phrase that ended just before its resolution? I'm sure you have. Perhaps you've heard someone play a musical scale, and they stopped before playing the final note. A sense of expectation and incompleteness happens when that phrase goes unresolved. Maybe it's annoying or irritating for you, perhaps even leaving you with an uncomfortable sensation in your body. I have seen comical videos on social media where someone, choosing to annoy musicians, plays a musical phrase and intentionally leaves it unresolved. And I have seen responses to those videos come in the form of the responder completing the musical phrase. I'm always amazed that when the musician completes the phrase, there is a bodily reaction—a smile, an exhale, a lowering of the shoulders. Resolutions feel good. The musicians can relax knowing all is once again right in the world because the musical phrase is resolved.

I know the resolution of my story is coming, but it is not here yet. And I'm going to assume you feel the same way. We need anchoring truths from scripture to keep us grounded as we await the resolution.

Here is a list of some of my anchoring scriptures:

Though he slay me, I will hope in him . . .
Job 13:15, ESV

*When the righteous cry for help, the LORD hears
and delivers them out of all their troubles. The
LORD is near to the brokenhearted and saves
the crushed in spirit.*
Psalm 34:17-18, ESV

*I am weary from my groaning;
with my tears I dampen my bed
and drench my couch every night.
My eyes are swollen from grief;
they grow old because of all my enemies.
Depart from me, all evildoers, for the
Lord has heard the sound of my weeping.
The Lord has heard my plea for help;
the Lord accepts my prayer.*
Psalm 6:6-9, CSB

*The Lord is a refuge for the persecuted,
a refuge in times of trouble.
Those who know your name trust in you
because you have not abandoned
those who seek you, Lord.*
Psalm 9:9-10, CSB

JOY IN THE MOURNING

How long, Lord? Will you forget me forever?
How long will you hide your face from me?
How long will I store up anxious concerns within me,
agony in my mind every day?
How long will my enemy dominate me?
Consider me and answer, Lord my God.
Restore brightness to my eyes;
otherwise, I will sleep in death.
My enemy will say, "I have triumphed over him,"
and my foes will rejoice because I am shaken.
But I have trusted in your faithful love;
my heart will rejoice in your deliverance.
I will sing to the Lord
because he has treated me generously.
Psalms 13, CSB

The law of the Lord is perfect, reviving the soul;
Psalm 19:7, ESV

For he has not despised or abhorred
the torment of the oppressed.
He did not hide his face from him
but listened when he cried to him for help.
Psalm 22:24, CSB

I will rejoice and be glad in your faithful love
because you have seen my affliction.
You know the troubles of my soul
and have not handed me over to the enemy.
You have set my feet in a spacious place.
Psalm 31:7-8, CSB

A Theology of Praise and Lament

Cast your burden on the Lord,
and he will sustain you;
he will never allow the
righteous to be shaken.
Psalm 55:22, CSB

You caused me to experience
many troubles and misfortunes,
but you will revive me again.
You will bring me up again,
even from the depths of the earth.
You will increase my honor
and comfort me once again.
Psalm 71:20-21, CSB

My flesh and my heart may fail,
but God is the strength of my heart
and my portion forever.
Psalm 73:26, ESV

Blessed are those whose strength is in you,
in whose heart are the highways to Zion.
As they go through the Valley of Baca (weeping)
they make it a place of springs; the early
rain also covers it with pools.
Psalm 84:5-6, ESV

You are good and do good;
Psalm 119:68, ESV

JOY IN THE MOURNING

Have you not known? Have you not heard?
The Lord is the everlasting God,
the Creator of the ends of the earth.
He does not faint or grow weary;
his understanding is unsearchable.
He gives power to the faint, and to
him who has no might he increases strength.
Even youths shall faint and be weary,
and young men shall fall exhausted; but they
who wait for the Lord shall renew their strength;
they shall mount up with wings like eagles;
they shall run and not be weary;
they shall walk and not faint.
Isaiah 40:28-31, ESV

Do not fear, for I am with you;
do not be afraid, for I am your God.
I will strengthen you; I will help you;
I will hold on to you with my
righteous right hand.
Isaiah 41:10, CSB

But this I call to mind,
and therefore I have hope:
The steadfast love of the Lord never ceases;
his mercies never come to an end;
they are new every morning;
great is your faithfulness.
"The Lord is my portion," says my soul,
"therefore I will hope in him."
Lamentations 3:21-24, ESV

A Theology of Praise and Lament

*Blessed be the God and Father of our Lord Jesus
Christ, the Father of mercies and the God of all
comfort. He comforts us in all our affliction, so that
we may be able to comfort those who are in any kind
of affliction, through the comfort we ourselves receive
from God. For just as the sufferings of Christ overflow
to us, so also through Christ our comfort overflows.*
2 Corinthians 1:3-5, CSB

*But he said to me, "My grace is sufficient
for you, for my power is perfected in weakness."*
2 Corinthians 12:9, CSB

*So then, let those who suffer according to God's will entrust
themselves to a faithful Creator while doing what is good.*
1 Peter 4:19, CSB

*He will wipe away every tear from their eyes. Death
will be no more; grief, crying, and pain will be no
more, because the previous things have passed away.*
Revelation 21:4, CSB

*We are afflicted in every way but not crushed; we
are perplexed but not in despair; we are persecuted
but not abandoned; we are struck down but not
destroyed. We always carry the death of Jesus in our body,
so that the life of Jesus may also be displayed in our body.*
2 Corinthians 4:8-10, CSB

*We do not want you to be uninformed, brothers and sisters,
concerning those who are asleep, so that you will not grieve
like the rest, who have no hope.*
1 Thessalonians 4:13, CSB

*Be sober-minded, be alert. Your adversary the devil
is prowling around like a roaring lion, looking for
anyone he can devour. Resist him, firm in the faith,
knowing that the same kind of sufferings are being
experienced by your fellow believers throughout the
world. The God of all grace, who called you to his
eternal glory in Christ, will himself restore,
establish, strengthen, and support you after
you have suffered a little while.*
1 Peter 5:8-10, CSB

*Therefore we do not give up. Even though our outer
person is being destroyed, our inner person is being
renewed day by day. For our momentary light
affliction is producing for us an absolutely incomparable
eternal weight of glory. So we do not focus on what
is seen, but on what is unseen. For what is seen
is temporary, but what is unseen is eternal.*
2 Corinthians 4:16-18, CSB

*Consider it a great joy, my brothers and sisters,
whenever you experience various trials, because
you know that the testing of your faith produces
endurance. And let endurance have its full effect,
so that you may be mature and complete,
lacking nothing.*
James 1:2-4, CSB

(13)

All of You

Grief affects the entirety of your being. Your mind. Your body. Your spirit. In the Hebrew perspective, the integration of all these components that make you you is called your soul. Therefore, grief affects your soul. In Chapter 5, The New Normal, I discussed creating a treatment plan or care package. Here I want to provide more context around this reality of grief affecting your soul and encourage you to consider ways to care for your soul well.

Mind

We've talked a little about the mind, but I want you to know you can change your life by changing how you think. The science is out, and we can celebrate the truth that we are neuroplastician. Neuroplasticity is the ability of neural networks in the brain to change through growth and reorganization. See the word plastic in there? This means your brain is pliable. Now, the mind is not the brain. The mind is non-tangible, but the brain is a tangible organ. The mind impacts and influences the brain, and you can use this truth to serve you well in grief.

As you continue on this journey, you have a choice in the narratives you believe. For the past few years, identity statements and affirmations have been a large part of my personal care package. For those wondering the difference, an identity statement is something true of who you are, and an affirmation is something you are growing, moving towards, or cultivating. For example, an identity statement might be *I am loved*. And an affirmation statement might be *Because I am loved, I walk in confidence and courage.*

A few years ago, I created a Google doc of more than 200 identity statements and affirmations in the categories of marriage, money, parenting, and more. I recorded all of these on my phone, resulting in a 12-minute voice memo! When possible, I listen to this recording first thing in the morning or right before I go to bed. It's a practice of speaking to myself (or listening to me speak to me) in a way that aligns with how God speaks to me and about me in various situations. This method has been an intentional practice of talking back to myself, setting my mind on things above, and I can feel the difference it has made in my life. I have been so moved by this practice that the first meeting I have with my doula clients is an affirmations creation session.

Now, this was not a practice in my first few years in grief. I did not have the capacity to sit down and create a list of 200 identity statements and affirmations. I could hold on to one or two statements, which I'd like to encourage you to do. Create one or two statements you can use on this journey. Here are some example statements created from reflections shared in part 2, knowing that affirmations can be created from the scriptures.

Identity statements

I am loved.
I am not alone.

Affirmations

I choose joy over despair.
I am honest with myself and others about where I am hurting.
I lean into the waves of sorrow.
I am hard-pressed on every side, but not crushed; per-

plexed, but not in despair; persecuted, but not abandoned; struck down, but not destroyed.

→Take a moment and create your own.

If you would like to go a little further in mindset work, here are some questions to guide you in determining stories, lies, or limiting beliefs that may not serve you well right now. Perhaps you will discover there is an opportunity to believe something new.

→Notice immediate responses or stories that come to mind when you consider the following topics. I have included some questions that may be helpful as you begin to notice what is there.

Identity

Questions - What do I believe about myself? What defines me? What is true about me?

Ex: I am defined by what I produce; I am what I do. I am a sinner and undeserving. I am an anxious person.

Mistakes

Questions - What do I believe about mistakes? How do I treat myself when I make a mistake? Are mistakes a part of life or unwelcome interruptions?

Ex: Mistakes are proof that I'm not perfect and are very uncomfortable to face. I am mean to myself when I make a mistake.

Rest

Questions - What do I believe about rest? How do I rest? Do I deserve rest? Why or why not?

Ex: I don't deserve rest, but I can earn it by working hard.

I can only rest after I've accomplished something. Rest comes after being productive.

Worth

Questions - Do I have worth? Why or why not? What determines my worth?

Ex: God has given me worth, but I often look to others to validate my worth.

Body

Questions - How do I feel about my body? What things do I say about my body?

Ex: My body is fearfully and wonderfully made, but I'm not happy with it. I want my body to look different.

Parenting

Questions - What do I believe about parenting? What do I believe about myself as a parent?

Ex: Parenting is hard. I want to be a perfect parent, but I know that's not realistic.

→Now that you've exposed what's there, notice if there is anything you'd like to change. If so, mark those items and use these follow-up questions:

Is it true?

Is this how God's voice sounds?

If not, am I willing to change it? Am I willing to believe something new?

What truths align with God's voice?

Craft a statement that serves you better.

Feel free to take as much time as you need to find verbiage that resonates and feels right for you. One final encouragement—craft your statements of identity and affirmation in the present tense (this is good for your subconscious).

Here's an example:

I'd like to change the default narrative —"I can only rest after I've accomplished something. Rest comes after being productive."

Is it true? *No*

Is this how God's voice sounds? *No*

If not, am I willing to change it? Am I willing to believe something new? *Yes.*

What truths align with God's voice? *God designed rest. God rested. Rest is a gift. God gives rest. Rest is a necessity because I am human.*

Craft a statement that serves you better. *I accept God's invitation to rest and remind myself I do not have to earn it through productivity.*

Body

I have found in certain church traditions, we forget about the body and overemphasize the mind. But it does not escape me that Christ put on flesh. It does not escape me that we are embodied beings. I am not just mind and spirit; part of my existence involves my body. Now, I am not only my body, and when I treat people as such, we call this objectification—minimizing someone's existence to only their physical body. To recap, I am not only my body. I am more than my body, but I am certainly not less than my body, which means I need to give some attention to my body.

The body is the common denominator of all the professional hats I wear. As a doula, I absolutely want you to connect with your body in pregnancy, labor, birth, postpartum, and beyond. In yoga and fitness classes, I guide students in various body movements to strengthen muscles and care well for our ligaments, tendons, and joints. Even in my wellness workshops and wellness coaching sessions, I will incorporate breath and body practices because I want the participants to have the lived experience of feeling a definite shift in their bodies.

The same is true for those in grief. I want you to know how to listen to and care for your body well so you can know deeper and greater healing. In my first week of grief, I got a grief massage, reflexology, and was gifted with essential oils. I was told to put this on my body to help my body deal with grief. I didn't understand why I needed this immediate emphasis on my body, but I trusted those around me and went with it.

One of the oils I was given was a blend called Joy, and to this day, I still rub it over my heart center daily. Years later, when I was reading about the flowers that made up this beautiful blend, I learned they all had properties supporting the body in various ways. One flower, in particular, helped a specific gland in the body to remain open when its natural response is to close during grief. And when this gland is open, it supports you in dealing with the physical realities that come with intense emotions. You may or may not be an essential oils fan, but I share this example because it communicates the truth that grief affects our bodies. I'm confident there are other effects of grief on my body if grief can cause a gland to close.

Let me give you a few encouragements to help your body process the grief because, just like the title of Ray Van der Kolk's incredible book, the body keeps the score.[19]

Sleep

I've heard that sleep is like taking your body to the repair shop. In our family, we often refer to it as a vitamin. It can be hard to find sleep in grief, but I want to encourage you to try.

Your body absolutely will need to go to the repair shop in grief. I used various essential oils, floral essences, and melatonin to promote sleep. As much as you can, try to get some sleep.

A great place to start is by taking slow deep breaths for at least two minutes when you lay down to go to bed. Allow your breaths to be so slow that you take 3 to 4 inhales every 60 seconds. (See Appendix B for more detailed breath practices.)

Here are a few other ideas to promote restful sleep:

- Use a sleep mask to block out potentially disturbing light.
- Play white, brown, or green noise to block out potentially disturbing sounds.
- Limit your exposure to white light 60 minutes before bed (using blue-blocking glasses is a great idea).
- Discontinue the use of screens 60 minutes before bed.

I recognize for some that sleep may be terrifying—as tragedy may have struck while you were sleeping. I'm sorry. This is not an easy place to be, and you are not alone. If you have a complicated relationship with sleep right now because of loss, be gentle with yourself. Consider taking moments throughout the day to promote your relaxation by using the breath practices in Appendix B. You could start with five minutes and work your way up to thirty. You may also consider adding a phrase like, "I am safe. It is safe to go to sleep." to your mindset work discussed earlier.

Move

I won't go into detail here about the states of the nervous system and completing stress cycles, but I will say moving is a great way to help your body deal with harmful stress. It could be stress as a result of grief or something else. If you're able, as often as you can, move your body in a way that raises your heart rate for a total of 30 minutes.

I recognize that 30 minutes of movement may feel overwhelming, so please know you can start with whatever feels right, a short walk, 10 jumping jacks, or 2 minutes with the punching bag. If you are working towards 30 minutes, it does not have to be consecutive. A 10-minute walk three times a day is a powerful practice. If you are facing grief, shielding well-intentioned but unhelpful comments from others, or being forced to learn a new lifestyle, you may already feel the pressure building in your body. Movement can be a therapeutic release valve.

The Vagus Nerve

Your vagus nerve is a part of your nervous system connecting your brain to every other organ in your body. You may have heard the phrase "toning your vagus nerve" or "improving your vagal tone." This refers to your nervous system's ability to deal with various situations—in both capacity and flexibility. I often say it's nice to have a pliable nervous system that can bend rather than break. Even if it feels broken, there are ways to mend it. There are ways to increase your nervous system's flexibility and capacity. Here's a short list of things you can do to support your vagus nerve and improve your vagal tone:

- Joint circles (circling wrists or ankles)
- Humming
- Buzzing (making a buzzing sound with your mouth)
- Rocking
- Singing

Ever notice how many of these items are soothing for babies? They are soothing for adults too.

Let me offer a quick personal story. I sang in my church's

gospel choir in my first year of grief. I didn't know why, but I would feel lighter after each rehearsal and church service singing in a group. I could not explain the relief. But I liked it, so I consistently went back to practice. I now know it was a combination of three things that were a gift to my nervous system and resulted in my lifted mood:

1. Singing
2. Being with other people
3. Participating in regulating rhythm (rocking and clapping)

I bet you can already think of an experience where you felt a boost from dancing or singing or doing these things in a group. If you can, do some of these while you're grieving.

For more encouragement on body postures and breath practices that can support you, see Appendix A & B.

Spirit

Dr. Anita Phillips conveys that the more healthy we are emotionally, the more powerful we are spiritually. All the previous words about caring for your mind and body influence your emotional health and by extension, your spiritual health. Of course, so much more could be said, but my encouragement here is simply to do the things that fuel your spirit. Maybe it's meditating on scripture or praying with people. If you're like me, I love to feel the sun's warmth on my skin as a reminder that God's face shines upon me (Numbers 6:25). Here are some questions to get your thoughts going:

- What stirs your affection for the Lord?
- What simple practices bring you joy?
- What simple practices help you feel closer to God?

- When do you feel closest to God?
- What makes you feel distant? (where possible, avoid these)

(14)

Words of Encouragement You Never Wanted to Hear

I would like to provide you with a more bite-sized version of my reflections. You can consider it a cheat sheet of encouragement to support you after a loss. Sometimes you don't have time for a long conversation; you just need a short text of encouragement from a friend.

This is that text.

My prayer for those who read this and my intention for writing is simply this:

Blessed be the God and Father of our Lord Jesus Christ, the Father of mercies and the God of all comfort. He comforts us in all our affliction, so that we may be able to comfort those who are in any kind of affliction, through the comfort we ourselves receive from God. For just as the sufferings of Christ overflow to us, so also through Christ our comfort overflows.
2 Corinthians 1:3-5, CSB

1. Despite what people may think or say, you have ___ kids (including your child who is safe in the arms of God).

2. It will be hard when people ask how many kids you have, but I encourage you to answer with your Child included in the number. It may feel weird when you don't.

3. You are not alone, though it may feel like it. Other parents have suffered similar losses, but no one knows EXACTLY how you feel. Your experience is unique because it's yours.

4. Try your best not to play "What If?" games. The hard truth is the Lord numbers our days, and there is nothing you could have done to change the outcome. God is the ultimate author of your and your child's story.

5. People will say well-intentioned, stupid stuff; if possible, don't take everything people share to heart.

6. Find a trusted group of people who can support you. It could be family, friends, a grief support group, etc. Fight against lies that may rob you of fellowship.

7. Know what touches you was first sifted through the Father's hand of love. This may be confusing and frustrating, but it is true.

8. Know you can simultaneously be a rejoicer and a mourner.

9. Counseling is a gift from God!

10. Trauma is real, and so is PTSD. You may find yourself easily triggered, and I pray that a counselor or loved one can help you determine things to serve you well when you are.

11. The silence of people can be deafening. People may

want to say things to you, but out of fear, they will keep silent. This is a terrible pain you shouldn't have to deal with.

12. The "new normal" is something you'll have to adjust to. You don't have to like it, but you will learn to adjust to it and accept it.

13. You will walk this journey for the rest of your life; I'm 10 years in, and I can tell you that, by the grace of the Lord, the intensity now is not what it was in the first year.

14. Time doesn't heal all wounds—only the God of all comfort can do that.

15. This has forever marked your soul. We may not be branded with a giant letter that identifies us as the grieving mom, but we have to accept this is a part of us now—not the whole of our identity, but a part.

16. Sorrow will sometimes come unexpectedly, like a wave; I encourage you to lean into the wave and feel what you need to feel. Yell, scream, cry, do nothing, etc.

17. If applicable, grieve with your spouse. You will probably grieve differently but try to do it together where possible.

18. The journey ahead may seem overwhelming, so be gentle with yourself. Take it slow— one day at a time. Scripture tells us God gives us new mercies daily, so exhaust the day's mercies and wake up tomorrow confident there will be more.

19. You may feel like you don't have enough energy to mourn your Child and deal with life's responsibilities, but you can say no to things.

20. There is no one way or right way to grieve. Feel free to grieve as you need and find healthy "release valves."

21. Your body will take a physical toll. I am convinced grief is a sickness, though most people won't understand this; as you heal, try to take care of yourself physically as best you can.

22. I call it a healing process because I don't think I'll ever have FULL healing here. When I'm in Heaven with Christ and Chase, I will be fully restored and healed; in the meantime, I'm taking this journey of restoration one day at a time.

23. Never feel the need to be "thankful" for this loss. I've heard parents say they were grateful for what they learned or the opportunities they had to minister to others through the loss of a child, but that DOES NOT mean they are thankful for the loss.

24. Asking for help is a refusal to give up; it is a show of strength.

25. Journaling was a beneficial exercise for me. I was able to write letters to Chase and write about my memories of him, hopes and dreams for him, etc. Maybe this will help you too.

26. We have an adversary who is against us even in hard times.

27. Try to care for yourself at every level—mind, body, and spirit. When you're ready, find ways to laugh; this is good medicine.

28. Settle in—this is a marathon. It may not be fun or easy, but it is possible to learn to get comfortable with the uncomfortable.

29. If you are caring for other children while grieving,

may these words from Brene Brown's Whole-Hearted Parenting Manifesto lay a foundation for your comfortable-in-the-uncomfortable support—"Together we will cry and face fear and grief. I will want to take away your pain, but instead, I will sit with you and teach you how to feel it."

30. You don't have to "get over this," "move on," or "let your child go."

Let me end with this powerful conversation between 2 vilomahs, bereaved parents, from the "Crisis Theory" episode of Westworld.[21]

Bereaved Dad: "When he died, I remember thinking it was like the sun had gone down . . . and it was never going to rise again. I walked in the dark for so long. I . . . can't let him go."

Bereaved Mom: "I never understood why people said that. If you love someone, why would you ever let them go? That's what saved me. The only part of [my son] I had left was his memory. And if I died [gave up], the darkness would take that, too. But if I kept moving, I could find the light again. And I could bring him with me."

Blessings to you as you go—and bring your child with you.

Appendix A - Postures

Here are descriptions of three postures you can use whenever you need a moment of stillness lying down. If a posture does not feel good or safe for you, feel free to make whatever adjustments your body needs to feel comfortable and safe.

For guided audio tracks to accompany you in postures of stillness please visit - www.wellwithdanielle.net/joyinthemourning

A list of props that can support you well in stillness:
- Workout/yoga mat
- Blanket(s)
- Pillows (of various shapes, sizes, and sturdiness)
- Eye mask or small towel

Relaxation Pose

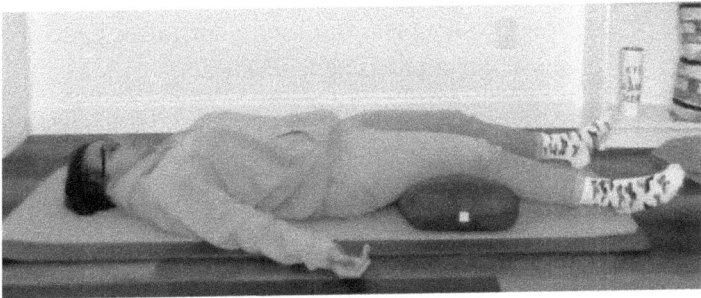

Relaxation Pose is lying down on the ground with your legs extended. It has several physical and emotional benefits, especially for those grieving. Physical benefits include: calming the central nervous system, aiding the digestive and immune systems, helps lower blood pressure. Emotional benefits include: calming the mind and reducing stress, reducing headache, fatigue, and anxiety, promotes spiritual awakening and awareness.

Recommended Props for Relaxation Pose: One pillow, mat, blanket, eye mask

1. Find an open space on the floor large enough for you to comfortably lie down.

2. Gently lie down on your back, allowing your chin to gently tilt towards your chest.

3. Notice how your body feels and make small adjustments to be more comfortable. (I like to place a small pillow under my knees to take tension off my lower back.)

4. Create space between your ankles, so there is space between your thighs.

5. Allow the feet and ankles to relax and naturally fall open.

6. Relax your arms down by your sides so there is space between your upper arms and your torso. Choose if palms down or palms up feel better.

7. Make any other small adjustments to the feet, legs, and rest of the body to promote your comfort.

8. Begin to deepen your breath, allowing the exhale to be longer than the inhale, to invite relaxation throughout your body.

9. Stay here for two to twenty minutes as it feels right for you.

Coming Out of Relaxation Pose
1. When you are ready to come out of the posture, invite gentle movement back to the body by wiggling the fingers and/or toes.
2. Slowly increase the size of the movements, perhaps circling wrists or ankles, or reaching arms overhead for a full body stretch.
3. Slowly roll to one side and begin to make your way up to a comfortable seated position.
4. Spend a few minutes journaling your experience.

Heart Opener

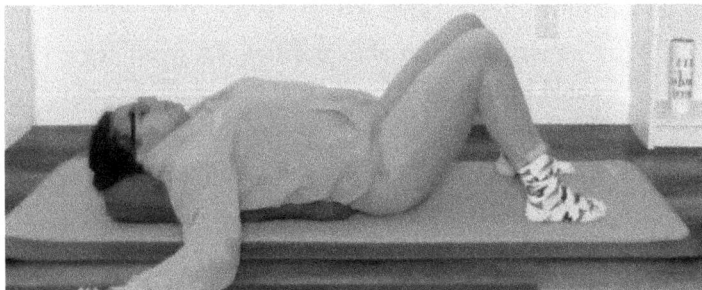

A heart-opening posture has several physical and emotional benefits, especially for those grieving. Physical benefits include: stretching the muscles in the chest and shoulders, releasing tension from the neck and shoulders, increases mobility and flexibility of the spine. Emotional benefits include: reducing stress and anxiety, decreasing feelings of aloneness, boosting feelings of self-confidence, increases openness to love.

Recommended Props for the Heart Opener: firm pillow, couch cushion or yoga bolster, yoga mat, blanket

1. Find an open space on the floor large enough for you

to comfortably lie down.

2. Position the pillow, cushion, or bolster* longways, so that it can support your spine while lying flat on your back.

3. Sit down on your bottom so the pillow, cushion, or bolster is behind you

4. Gently lie down on the pillow, cushion, or bolster. (If you're using a blanket for warmth, be sure to place it on top of your legs before you lie down.)

5. Choose a comfortable position for your arms. (Your hands could be near your hips or you could extend your arms out to the side straight, or with elbows bent.)

6. Choose a comfortable position for your legs. (You could bend the knees while allowing the feet to rest on the floor, or straighten your legs along the floor.)

7. Make any other small adjustments to the feet, legs, and rest of the body to promote your comfort.

8. Begin to deepen your breath, allowing the exhale to be longer than the inhale, to invite relaxation throughout your body.

9. Stay here for two to twenty minutes as it feels right for you.

*If practicing without a pillow, cushion, or bolster, lie flat on your back and squeeze your shoulder blades together underneath you, while keeping your head on the ground.

Coming Out of the Heart Opener
1. When you are ready to come out of the posture, invite gentle movement back to the body by wiggling the fingers and/or toes.

2. Slowly increase the size of the movements, perhaps circling wrists or ankles, or reaching arms overhead for a full body stretch.

3. Slowly roll to one side and begin to make your way up to a comfortable seated position.

4. Spend a few minutes journaling your experience.

Hip Opener

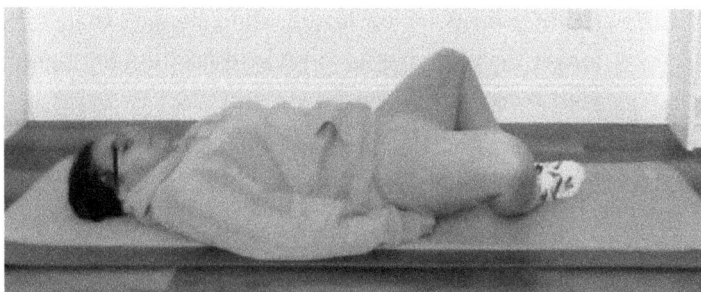

A hip-opening posture has several physical and emotional benefits, especially for those grieving. Physical benefits include: stretching the muscles in the hips, releasing tension from the spine and lower back, promotes hip and body alignment. Emotional benefits include: releasing stored emotions, promoting feelings of freedom, increases clarity and creativity.

Recommended Props for the Hip Opener: Two flexible pillows, yoga mat, blanket

1. Find an open space on the floor large enough for you to comfortably lie down.

2. Gently lie down on your back, knees bent toward the ceiling, and feet resting on the floor. (If you're using a blanket for warmth, be sure to place it on top of your

legs before you lie down.)

3. Slowly begin to open your knees so that the bottoms of the feet can touch.

4. Allow the knees to open as wide as they are able.

5. If desired, use props to support the legs. You can place a folded pillow under each thigh or knee, or rest your fists on the outer part of your hips, near your glutes.

6. Make any other small adjustments to the feet, legs, and rest of the body to promote your comfort.

7. Begin to deepen your breath, allowing the exhale to be longer than the inhale, to invite relaxation throughout your body.

8. Stay here for two to twenty minutes as it feels right for you.

Coming Out of the Hip Opener

1. When you are ready to come out of the posture, invite gentle movement back to the body by wiggling the fingers and/or toes.

2. Place your hands under your thighs and gently support your legs as you bring your knees together, closing the legs and hips.

3. Slowly increase the size of the movements, perhaps circling wrists or ankles, or reaching arms overhead for a full body stretch. It may even feel nice to hug both knees in towards the chest as if you're curling up into a ball.

4. Slowly roll to one side and begin to make your way up to a comfortable seated position.

5. Spend a few minutes journaling your experience.

Appendix B - Breath Practices

Here are descriptions of breath practices you can use whenever you need a moment of calm. These practices are meant to help stimulate your body's parasympathetic nervous system, which activates your relaxation response.

For guided audio tracks please visit - www.wellwithdanielle.net/joyinthemourning

4-8 Breathing

1. Find a comfortable seated position and begin to deepen your breath by taking air in through the nostrils and sighing it out your open mouth.

2. Repeat Step 1 three times.

3. Seal your lips and begin to take air in through your nostrils for a slow count of 4.

4. Exhale the air out the nostrils to a slow count of 8.

5. Repeat Steps 3 & 4 three times.

Inhale & Long Exhale

1. Find a comfortable seated position and begin to deepen your breath by taking air in through the nostrils and

sighing it out your open mouth.

2. Repeat Step 1 three times.

3. Seal your lips and slowly take air in through your nostrils (no need to count).

4. As slow as possible, gently begin to release the air through your pursed/puckered lips (imagine you're trying to gently cool off a bowl of soup in such a way that the soup doesn't splash onto your face).

5. Repeat Steps 3 & 4 three times.

Inhale - Exhale - Hold (Triangle Breathing)

1. Find a comfortable seated position and begin to deepen your breath by taking air in through the nostrils and sighing it out your open mouth.

2. Repeat Step 1 three times.

3. Seal your lips and begin to take air in through your nostrils for a slow count of 4.

4. Exhale the air out the nostrils to a slow count of 8.

5. After the air is fully expelled, pause for a slow count of 4.

6. Repeat Steps 3, 4 & 5 three times.

Appendix C - At Home Labyrinth Practice

What is a Labyrinth?

A labyrinth is a complex and circular path that leads from a starting point to a center. Some refer to labyrinths as a maze, but in my understanding and experience a labyrinth is a single, undivided path. These are sometimes referred to as a meandering labyrinth. Staying on this undivided path always leads one to the center—the assured goal.

In the Middle Ages, not everyone could make the long journey to the Holy Land, so walking a labyrinth became a substitute for the pilgrimage to Jerusalem. It was viewed as a devotional activity. Today meandering labyrinths are used in a variety of ways, two of which are for prayer and meditation.

I hope you find this finger labyrinth helpful on your journey.

Using a Labyrinth for Prayer

1. Practice the Presence of God - Remind yourself God is with you as you trace the path. Ask for the grace to stay mindful of His presence.

2. Set your intention - If you have any particular intentions on your mind, name them and "carry" them with

you as you trace. For example, your intention could be to focus on the truth "I am loved."

3. Trace the path - Begin and trace the path knowing God is with you. Go at a pace that feels right for you. As you trace, notice what happens in your mind. Does the mind drift? That's OK, simply bring it back to your intention.

4. Practice Gratitude - When you reach the center of the labyrinth, practice gratitude for God being and staying with you, reminding yourself that God will not leave or forsake you.

5. Reflect - Afterwards, take time to reflect. Write down your thoughts, feelings, or anything else you experienced.

If you enjoyed the practice of tracing a labyrinth, consider walking a labyrinth. Find labyrinths in your area here - https://labyrinthlocator.com/

Appendix D - Books and Other Resources

Books

- Heaven by Randy Alcorn
- From Grief to Glory by James W. Bruce III
- The One Year Book of Hope by Nancy Guthrie
- Walking with God through Pain and Suffering - Tim Keller
- Prophetic Lament - Soong-Chan Rah
- A Grace Disguised: How the Soul Grows through Loss - Jerry Sittser

Resources

- www.griefshare.org - You can sign up to receive daily emails, they also have groups around the country that you can join (I didn't join a group, but have heard great things about them).
- http://mend.org/support/ - M.E.N.D - Mothers Enduring Neonatal Death

For more resources, please visit www.wellwithdanielle.net/joyinthemourning

Chase

Lyrics by Tedashii

I will go chasing you

Trusting you

Hope in you

Forever, forever, oh

When I first held you I cried

If I would have known a year later I wouldn't have you in this life

I would've never let you go, just held you close

One of the few things that really mattered to me most

Seems unfair how life treats us down here

We grow attached to the very people that can disappear

I would do anything to have you back again

One more smile, just one more kiss

To hear you cry when you don't get your way

I never knew to cherish that and now it seems too late

At least it feels that way, how I'll never forget

How I'll keep holding on until I see you again

You give, and you take, through it all I will chase after your heart

Not your head, when my heart don't understand

I will go chasing you

Trusting you

Hope in you

Forever, forever, oh

I will go chasing you

Trusting you

Hope in you

Forever, forever, oh

In the morning I would play with you

Your smile would be the only thing to help me make it through

So many things I want to say to you

But I guess that Heaven couldn't wait for you

I dreamed of a life that would last past mine

Now when I wake up I wish that I could stop time

He gives and takes away, what more can I say?

I just trust and hope that he'll make everything ok

I know there's never been a day that he didn't love me

Even now it's hard to see, but he's there above me

And every time I think about it I know you're with him

So I keep holding on until I see you again

You give, and you take, through it all I will chase after your heart

Not your head, when my heart don't understand

I will go chasing you

Trusting you

Hope in you

Forever, forever, oh

I will go chasing you

Trusting you

Hope in you

Forever, forever, oh

I will go chasing you

Trusting you

Hope in you

Forever, forever, oh

Notes

1. Holloway, Karla. "A Name for a Parent Whose Child Has Died." Duke Today. Accessed March 24, 2023. https://today.duke.edu/2009/05/holloway_oped.html.

2. Bruce, James W. *From Grief to Glory: Spiritual Journeys of Mourning Parents*. Edinburgh U.K.: Banner of Truth Trust, 2008.

3. Donney, Laura. Episode. *WandaVision* 1, no. 8- Previously On. Accessed May 8, 2023. Disney+.

4. Menakem, Resmaa. "Chapter 1: Your Body and Blood." Essay. In *My Grandmother's Hands: Racialized Trauma and the Pathway to Mending Our Hearts and Bodies*. London: Penguin Books, 2021.

5. Spurgeon, C. H., and Roy H. Clarke. *Beside still waters: Words of comfort for the soul*. Nashville, TN: T. Nelson Publishers, 1999.

6. Lewis, Clive S. *The problem of pain*. Glasgow: Collins, 1983.

7. dailyemails@griefshare.org. *Day 283 - Learning Through Grief,* January 8, 2014.

8. Descartes, René, and John Veitch. *A discourse on method.* London: Dent, 1953.

9. Boom, Corrie Ten. *The Hiding Place by Corrie Ten Boom*. New York, : Bantam, 1974.

10. *Dr. Strange in the Multiverse of Madness*. USA: Marvel Studios, 2022.

11. Gorrell, Angela Williams, and Miroslav Volf. The gravity of joy: A story of being lost and found. Grand Rapids, MI: William B. Eerdmans Publishing Company, 2021.

12. Thompson, Dr. Curt, Angulus Wilson, Steve Beers, and Morgan C. Feddes. "Shining Light on Shame - Combating the Effects of Shame." CCCU, April 2017. https://www.cccu.org/magazine/shining-light-shame/.

13. Alcorn, Randy C. *Heaven*. Carol Stream, IL: Tyndale House Publishers, 2008.

14. Willie Jennings. "Joy and the Act of Resistance Against Despair," 2021, in *For the Life of the World*, produced by Miroslav Volf, Matthew Croasmun, Ryan McAnnally-Linz, Drew Collins, and Evan Rosa, podcast, mp3, 25, https://faith.yale.edu/media/joy-and-the-act-of-resistance-against-despair#:~:text=Willie%20Jennings%3A%20I%20look%20at,become%20a%20way%20of%20life.

15. Milicia, Gina. "A comfort zone is a beautiful place, but nothing ever grows there." Gina Milicia (blog). January 24, 2017. https://www.ginamilicia.com/blog/a-comfort-zone-is-a-beautiful-place-but-nothing-ever-grows-there/#:~:text=A%20comfort%20zone%20is%20a,ever%20grows%20there%20%2D%20Gina%20Milicia

16. *The Shack*. Directed by Stuart Hazeldine. 2017. Santa Monica, CA: Summit Entertainment, 2017. DVD.

17. Rah, Soong-Chan. *Prophetic lament: A Call for Justice in*

Troubled Times. Downers Grove, IL: IVP Books, an imprint of InterVarsity Press, 2015.

18. Rah, Soong-Chan. Prophetic lament: A call for justice in troubled Times. Downers Grove, IL: IVP Books, an imprint of InterVarsity Press, 2015

19. Van der Kolk, Bessel. *The Body Keeps the Score: Mind, Brain and Body in the Transformation of Trauma*. UK: Penguin Books, 2015.

20. Brown, Brené. "The Wholehearted Parenting Manifesto." Brené Brown, October 31, 2021. https://brenebrown.com/resources/the-wholehearted-parenting-manifesto/.

21. "Westworld/ Crisis Theory." Episode. *Westworld* 3, no. 8, May 3, 2020.

Acknowledgements

I'd like to express my gratitude for those who have not only been instrumental in the process of writing this book, but in my life as a whole. That said, I'd like to start with my mom, Sheila. Thank you for your presence and faithfulness, always. I am forever grateful for your encouragement and support - thank you for gifting your grandsons with the same. You had a unique burden: grieving the loss of your grandson while watching your daughter grieve the loss of her son. You are seen and you are loved. To my sister, Kristen, thank you for always being a voice of encouragement and for bearing burdens too heavy for me to carry alone. To my grandmother, Mimi, thank you for teaching me trust in the power and goodness of God through the beauty of creation. To my aunt, Lisa, thank you for being an example of vulnerability and always encouraging me to keep going. To my brother, Jason, thank you for your steady presence and tender power. To my dad, Paul, thank you for always believing in me and for capturing life in photos. Thank y'all for making sure I never walk this journey alone.

To my husband, Tedashii, thank you for faithfully walking this journey with me–same team. To the young man that was the first to call me mom, Jaden, thank you for your courage & vulnerability as we've walked this path–may you continue to walk in that for the good of humanity. To Chase, so much of what I do now is in your honor–I hope I'm making you proud–until that day. To Callen, the one who grew in my belly in the beginning of grief, thank you for your steadfastness and curiosity–may you be a force in the world that shows others the true Rock. To Kai, my fourth son, thank you for bringing a contagious energy and joy to every space you enter, bless you as you keep bringing restoration.

To my friends who have journeyed alongside me since the beginning of grief - Tricia, Johana & Chris, Dawntoya & Adam, Vanja, Lydia, Ashley. Thank you for your constant presence and for holding up my arms when I didn't have the strength.

To Chariti and Luke's Mom - thank you for caring for me as you navigated your own experience in "the unimaginable." Your love, support, validation and words of wisdom have forever changed my life–bless you for comforting me with the comfort you received.

To the team at United House Publishing, thank you for your partnership in getting these words out of my head and into the world.

To my readers - thank you for picking up this book and trusting me to share. I pray my words speak life into you.

To my younger self - thank you for not giving up. Thank you for choosing to care for your baby by caring for you. I believe that choice will impact generations - thank you for your courage to make it.

To my Divine Mother-Father, Adonai, The Great Spirit, Ha'Shem - I know You are good and in control, so I put my trust in You. Thank you for being with me, for believing in me, for enabling me to tread on the heights. Thank You for knowing & loving me.

About the Author

Danielle Anderson is a trauma-informed author, speaker, and wellness coach. She is amazed by God's beautiful and complex mind-body-spirit design of humans and is on a mission to share wellness practices that help others pursue whole health–mental, physical, emotional & spiritual. She believes this leads to more life to the full and becoming agents of healing in our circles of influence.

As a speaker, she has supported several organizations with her Signature Wellness Offerings, including Reach Records, the Lady Hawks, and Truth's Table. Other writing credits include contributions to His Testimonies, My Heritage - Women of Color on the Word of God and Joy in the Sorrow. As a doula and embodiment practitioner, Danielle believes in tapping into the wisdom of the body as a way to more fully know, and be known by, our Faithful Creator.

A self-proclaimed gummy bear snob, Danielle believes in finding joy in the simple - enjoying a movie, reading a book in the sunlight, or calming down with some slow flow yoga. She and her husband, Tedashii, live in Atlanta, GA and are the proud parents of 4 beautiful boys. To join her community and enjoy wellness encouragements, visit www.wellwithdanielle.net.

Stay Connected with Danielle
wellwithdanielle.net
Instagram @danielle.l.anderson

Milton Keynes UK
Ingram Content Group UK Ltd.
UKHW022134251124
451529UK00013B/836

9 781952 840555